M

I

N

M

I

THE NEW SIMPLICITY IN GRAPHIC DESIGN
STUART TOLLEY

Still life photography by Stuart Tolley
over 400 illustrations

N

CONTENTS

PRODUCTION

Print production used as a replacement for graphic design
as a method for communication

GEOMETRY

Simplifying design to its purest graphic form using shape
and abstract compositions to create bold graphic designs

INTRODUCTION

██████████

Minimalism is not a trend. It's an enduring visual discipline that has influenced every facet of visual culture, including art, architecture, industrial design, photography, music, fashion and graphic design. It's a form of restraint that comes to the fore as a reaction to overtly ornate and expressive graphic trends, often during times of social flux. Exemplified in the phrase 'Less is More', originally coined by the poet Andrea del Sarto in 1855 and later adapted by the minimalist architect Ludwig Mies van der Rohe, simplification is a process to cleanse the visual landscape.

MIN is an exploration of the new wave of pared-back graphic design, geometric forms and crafted production that has emerged after a decade in which decorative visual trends and 'bling' culture have held sway. The book is a showcase of classic, considered and restrained graphic design that places reduction, not decoration, at the heart of creation.

Reduction The opening section of MIN explores how restraint and reduction are applied by graphic designers. The essential ingredient is, traditionally, white space – reducing design to its most basic ingredient: white paper or screen. But there is more to reduction. This section also explores how graphic designers crop, abstract and manipulate images to create original compositions.

Production The revival of tactile print production for graphic design has been prevalent for several years and can largely be attributed to the oversaturation of digital formats. People still love to hold a beautiful object in their hands. It's human. This section of the book explores how production has superseded, and even replaced, graphic design decoration as a means of communication.

Geometry Simplifying design to its purest graphic form while still conveying a concept is the essence of geometric graphic design. This is achieved using abstract shapes and compositions to create bold patterns, often combined with striking colour palettes.

The public perception that minimalism is the easy option originated in the 1950s and early 1960s. A new visual language centred around restraint and order was pioneered by innovators such as the American artist Frank Stella, who wanted art to be viewed literally as an object in its own right, free from art-historical connotations. Stella began to experiment with visual restriction, and the resulting work manifested itself in his earliest abstract minimal explorations, *Black Paintings*, exhibited at the Museum of Modern Art in New York in 1959. This series, consisting of four exhibited paintings, featured precise black parallel geometric stripes, painted using ordinary household paint smoothly applied. This approach, intended to emphasize the flatness of the canvas, was conceived to make the viewer aware that a painting is a two-dimensional object. Aside from cementing Stella as a celebrated artist, the series also provided inspiration for a new style of art called minimalism.

This new approach to creating art was revolutionary and at odds with traditional art based upon the visualization of landscapes, religious symbols, nature and portraiture. Stella encapsulated his new style with the phrase 'what you see is what you see', coined to describe the work that expressed his goal of changing the modern perception of traditional art. Pop Art, which emerged in the mid-1950s, also afforded contemporary artists the space to look at artworks as objects in their own right and reject themes normally associated with traditional fine art such as morality, mythology, landscape and classical history. Both artistic styles contributed to the public perception that 'anyone can do that', but, unlike minimalism, Pop Art was eventually embraced by the public. This can largely be attributed to its populist subject matter and appearance in commercial formats such as album covers.

But history has not always been kind to minimalism. The American minimalist artist Carl Andre helped cement the public perception that 'anyone can do that'. In 1966 Andre created the *Equivalent* series, a set of eight structures with the same height, mass and volume but in different shapes, which are therefore all 'equivalent'. *Equivalent VIII*, the last in the series, was a sculptural artwork made from 120 standard household bricks arranged on the floor in two layers, in a six-by-ten rectangle. This artwork later became known as 'the pile of bricks' after it was bought by the Tate Gallery in London in 1972. There was public outrage at the time about the fee paid by the Tate for the artwork, which culminated in the *Daily Mirror* newspaper proclaiming, 'what a load of rubbish'. The work of art has since become a by word for the perceived pretentiousness of abstract art, which has been hard to shrug off ever since.

MIN aims to dispel some of these clichés, illustrating that a simplified approach to graphic design is far from the easy option and can take years to master through endless refinement and restraint. For the majority of contributors to this book, this approach to graphic design is more than an adopted style – it is a statement of intent. 'Simplify to clarify', as the strategic brand and graphic design studio BVD proclaim.

I believe it takes much more discipline for graphic designers to reduce their visual direction and, in particular, to abstain from visual trends which date quickly than to add decoration. For over a decade the dominant visual trend has leant towards ornamental graphic design and decorative illustrated swooshes inspired by calligraphy.

We all recognize the style, which is often applied to advertisements that sell anything from cars to beauty products, and adorns book covers, packaging and magazines. In the right hands it can look beautiful, but it is pure decoration and often badly parodied. Ornamental styles can also appear as if they are trying too hard. You only need to look at the barrage of overly complicated and ornate information graphics to see this: the message is lost in the design. The role of information graphics is to communicate complex information through data visualization, but in over-zealous hands it can result in a complicated mess of miscommunication. This is a classic example of style over substance.

A move towards simplification can be a barometer for social change and it is important to view minimalist works through the eyes of history in order to avoid misinterpretation. There is a rich and often anarchic background to simplification; a series of essays on the topic punctuates this book. Each reflects a pivotal moment in society, where a simplified visual language was utilized and echoed social change.

This is indeed true today. The move towards a simplified approach to graphic design is a reflection of our society, which is dominated by global austerity and cuts to social services, and echoes the earlier development of an abstract, minimal approach to the visual arts over a century ago. As discussed in the essay on 'Social Revolution' in this book, this development was attributed to the Russian Suprematist painter Kazimir Malevich. His seminal artwork *Black Square*, created in 1915, was exactly as the title suggests: a black square painted onto a white canvas. It expressed Malevich's desire to revolutionize art, moving away from representation. It was a monumental painting and inspired a plethora of other visual art styles and graphic designers alike. Contemporary society is now desensitized to this style, but at the time it shocked the art world because of its modern, machine-inspired aesthetic. Never before had painting been simplified so far.

This was a period of unparalleled creative innovation, and a time when artists believed their work would inspire social and political revolution. This seems naive now, in our visually sophisticated society, but graphic design was a powerful tool for organizing social change. The graphic languages of sub-cultures and human rights movements during the 20th century show this, but the role of the visual communicator has changed significantly since then.

This change was most evident in the 1950s, when the modern graphic designer was born. Before this period graphic design did not have its own unified modern visual language and was instead an amalgamation of styles all vying for attention. It seems obvious now, but design is a tool for communication and it was not until the introduction of a reduced graphic style centred around the grid systems, as discussed in the essay on 'The Grid', that this new modern era had a consistent visual direction. It was also during this time that a newer form of communication occupied the role of the graphic designer. This was nowhere more evident than in America, where the rise of consumerism in the 1950s meant products had to catch the consumer's eye. This meant the birth of a new role for the graphic designer, as discussed in the 'Excess Meets Less' essay. During this period a sophisticated minimal visual language was created that was designed to cut through the visual noise of design and was at odds with everything that had preceded it. Consumers bought into this lifestyle wholesale and

'A move towards simplification can be a barometer for social change and it is important to view minimalist works through the eyes of history in order to avoid misinterpretation. There is a rich and often anarchic background to simplification.'

advertisers fed on that as it became evident that the less-is-more approach to graphic design was an effective tool for communication.

It is important to analyse the history of graphic design, but *MIN* isn't retro. Some featured projects have been influenced by the minimalist graphic styles already discussed, but this book aims to offer a fresh perspective on contemporary simplification; for this reason the recent swathe of re-imagined graphic film posters, book covers and personal projects created in a minimalist style has not been included. Examples were selected for their beautifully considered, timeless, restrained graphic design.

Each of the case studies has been photographed exclusively for this book in a still-life environment. This creates a consistent visual platform so the reader can enjoy the work. The central focus is the objects themselves, not the design framework. To emphasize this, a suitably pared-back photographic style has been adopted, using a crisp and cool colour palette that utilizes two variations of semi-reflective Fedrigoni papers. These papers were chosen because they reduce the interference of shadows and create a continual horizontal line that flows through the pages of the book to create calm and balance.

To gain further insight into the simplified approach to graphic design, the three sections are each opened by an exclusive in-depth interview accompanied by specially commissioned portrait photography. Each of the interviewees was specifically chosen because their working philosophy typifies the new wave of simplified graphic design. Each interview is centred around their simplified visual direction, but also delves deeper into why a minimalist visual approach has been employed and how this is relevant in today's working environment.

In the essay 'Simplification Today' the idea of simple living is explored. We have a choice about whether or not we immerse ourselves in technology. We are constantly being bombarded with information, whether we want it or not, and I believe it is important to seek calm in our modern, constantly switched-on lives. *MIN* is designed to be enjoyed over a period of time and, not too dissimilar to vinyl records, encourages immersing yourself in the subject.

So sit back, switch off your mobile devices and enjoy.

REDUC

T

ION

C E R E A L

Interview Matthew Lee **Photograph** Ivan Jones

Cereal is a biannual travel and style magazine founded in Bristol by Rosa Park and Rich Stapleton. It was launched in 2012 as a quarterly publication with a print run of 3,000 and was quickly acclaimed for its innovative structure, distinctive photography and minimalist design. More recently, the duo have launched a series of city guides. They live together in Bath.

How did Cereal come about?

ROSA: I love magazines and I've collected them since I was young, but I never thought that one day I'd make my own. And if I hadn't met Richard it never would have happened. We both realized that we wanted to start over in a creative way – that was how we initially bonded.

RICH: I did a master's degree in engineering, but I was always visually oriented and wanted to focus on the design side of things.

ROSA: Rich got a job at a creative agency and I got a job at a local Bath magazine, which he worked on regularly as a photographer. We were soon collaborating quite a bit, creating all this content and wondering where it could go next. At first *Cereal* was a bit of a joke, but it soon got serious. I secured funding for it up front and then there was no turning back. I quit my job for the launch, but Rich worked for another nine months.

Which magazines or brands inspired the concept?

ROSA: In terms of magazines, I have a lot of admiration for *Monocle*, as does everybody else. *The Gentlewoman* is fantastic too. *Monocle* inspired me to look outside the mainstream glossy magazine world and it remains the only magazine I subscribe to. I admire it as a business and the way it's built its brand. Like *Monocle*, we have our magazine at the forefront of everything we do, but now we also have our city guides, the products we create working with other brands, and we're working towards opening physical stores. I'd say our biggest design inspiration is the Japanese retailer Muji, the 'brandless brand'. When you walk into a Muji store there's not a single branded element and yet you know it's a world that Muji created. We want to emulate the ethos of the brandless brand, a feeling that you know is *Cereal*. It will take time to achieve it, but that's the goal.

What challenges did you face when creating the first issue?

ROSA: We'd talked so much about the topics we wanted to cover and the writers and photographers we wanted to work with that the first issue came together pretty quickly. We had around 40 contributors, which is nuts because now we only work with around ten. It was such a big investment in terms of time and money and it was exhausting because we didn't have much experience in editorial. I'm almost loathe to say the word 'timeless', but we wanted the articles to have a timeless quality. It's about long-form journalism, and writing about things that are still interesting in a few years' time.

How were you able to convince so many experienced writers and photographers to work for a magazine that didn't yet exist?
ROSA: Well, we paid them what they wanted. People always ask what my advice is for starting an independent magazine and I always say 'money' – you need money to get it off the ground. We also invested in some heavy PR for our launch.

How did you choose the destinations you covered?
ROSA: There's a logic to how we picked them. There's a major city, a lesser-known city – like Bristol or Antwerp – and a far-flung destination like Yukon or the Moroccan desert. We always try to find the *Cereal* in every destination. It's easier to do that in some cities – Scandinavia is like a dream for us – but we struggle a bit where the urban aesthetic isn't generally in keeping with our style.

Your tagline has changed from 'Travel and Lifestyle' to 'Travel and Style'. Did this change mark a shift of focus?
ROSA: Yes, because style includes lifestyle – fashion, people, architecture, design, books, food. It's the whole nine yards of the word 'style' and it gives us a bit more freedom.

It seems you established the Cereal aesthetic – functional design, neutral tones, minimal clutter – in that very first issue.
RICH: Our perspective and photograph style have remained pretty consistent from volume one through to the latest volume – neutral tones, expansive landscapes, clean interiors, product and lifestyle shots.
ROSA: Some people have strong opinions on this aesthetic. Some people love minimalism, others hate it. Some people hate neutral tones and love lots of colour. But I can only be around neutral things because I'm a very chaotic, all-over-the-place kind of person so I maintain my sanity by keeping myself in a very calm, neutral setting, and that's the world that becomes *Cereal*. Richard is naturally a calm, laid-back guy and his tastes are a natural reflection of that.

Apart from the photography you do yourselves, everything you publish is commissioned. Is it a challenge getting that distinctive Cereal aesthetic from contributors?
RICH: We give extremely detailed briefs. Say we're doing a piece on candles, I will amass images of candles, textures, smoke and everything to give them a colour palette, a style, a shot list, angles, everything. And if need be, I'll be on set to guide them through it.
ROSA: Everything is so tightly controlled because it has to fit into the world that we're creating.
RICH: We approach the magazine in an interesting way. We plan the entire volume before we shoot anything. We decide the topics and the features and then choose photographers

and writers we think will do what's required. That's why our 40 contributors have been whittled down to around ten. We found the people we're on the same wavelength with.

Why aren't there any people in your photography?

ROSA: I think *Cereal* is a solitary experience, a solo reading experience. There are no human beings in our photographs unless we're doing an interview and even then it's usually a side profile. The reader's perception of a person in a photo affects how they perceive the entire photo, in a good or bad way. And with our landscape imagery we want you to imagine yourself there and we don't want anyone else to get in the way.

Why do you have so much white space on your pages?

RICH: It's important to us that the images and words have as much breathing space as possible, even if that means sacrificing valuable print space. Obviously paper is expensive, a premium product, but we want the images to be shown in their best light, and the same with the words. It means people can feel a bit more calm and relaxed when they flick through the volume.

ROSA: A lot of people tell us that *Cereal* is really peaceful and that's fantastic. That's what we want.

RICH: We want it to be the opposite of busy. People often talk about the design of *Cereal*. But the design of *Cereal* is that there is no design. We always want the words and the photos to take centre stage.

ROSA: Exactly. The design is there only to serve the words and the images.

Over time it seems the design has become more minimalist. There's a constant process of stripping back...

ROSA: Those tiny adjustments and iterations can make a huge difference. We're always refining it. It's always about functionality – if something isn't doing anything, take it out. We're definitely not in the ornamentation camp.

RICH: There's a quote I always think of that Rosa hates: 'Perfection is not when there's nothing left to add, it's when there's nothing left to take away.'

ROSA: I'm always wary that minimalism can sometimes look cold and austere. I think the Scandinavians and the Japanese tend to do a good job of being simple and minimal but with plenty of warmth. That's the kind of minimalism we go for.

RICH: As I come from an engineering background I approach design in a very organized way. It's all based on grids, order, symmetry...

ROSA: Rich is obsessed with symmetry! There's a sense of rigidity to *Cereal*. There's a rigorous process, a backbone, a structure.

Why did you remove the lines between the letters on your logo?

ROSA: The thin lines between the letters of the original logo were there to emulate the lines of books on a bookshelf. It was an ode to our love of books as well as a hope that our readers would collect *Cereal* and line it up on their bookshelves. They were removed in the most recent redesign

'I'm always wary that minimalism can sometimes look cold and austere. I think the Scandinavians and Japanese tend to do a good job of being simple and minimal but with plenty of warmth. That's the kind of minimalism we go for.'

as we refined the overall look and feel of *Cereal*. Rich and I are on a constant path to refining and distilling. If something doesn't serve a specific purpose then we often take that element away, piece by piece. Taking away the lines was part of that process. I think we are drawn to simplicity more and more as time goes by.

Are you drawn to this logic, order and simplicity when you visit and create content on cities?

RICH: That minimalist aesthetic exists everywhere, as does chaos. If you look at the world in general, especially nature, it's an ordered place. Look at the seascape, the sand dunes – they're very geometric, very symmetrical. Cities are quite orderly too; they are designed by architects, who are usually interested in symmetry and that kind of thing.

Why do you print on uncoated paper?

RICH: If it was printed on shiny, glossy paper and it was minimalist it would feel a little colder. I think you get some warmth out of the texture of the paper. Uncoated paper is notoriously difficult because it knocks everything back. It's unpredictable and it's more muted. It can be difficult with artworks which are high contrast and sharp because that can get lost on uncoated paper.

You do the design and much of the photography and writing yourselves, as well as running a growing business. How do you manage your schedule?

RICH: And we've been to every single location featured in the magazine so we can personally vouch for everything in there.

ROSA: It's pretty intense. We have no concept of weekends and evenings. We work every day, night and day. But you gotta do what you gotta do.

You live together and work together. Do you ever stop thinking about Cereal?

RICH: There isn't a day we don't create content. With social media there's always something to update so we constantly think about *Cereal* and we view the world through a *Cereal* lens.

ROSA: We work together but we're also together together. And it's a business we created together from the ground up so I don't think there's anything wrong with always thinking about it.

Even Sunday mornings in bed?

ROSA: Yeah, even then. But I've made my peace with it because I love what we do.

Rosa Park and Rich Stapleton were photographed at the Holburne Museum, Bath, UK

ROSA PARK & RICH STAPLETON
CEREAL

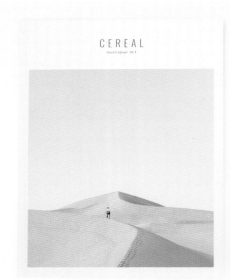

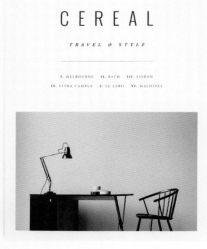

Published biannually, *Cereal* is an independent travel and style magazine at the forefront of the new wave of independent publishing that has helped breathe new life into the industry.

Created by editor and publisher Rosa Park and creative director Rich Stapleton, the magazine is recognizable for its quietly confident and understated approach to editorial design and photography, along with carefully curated editorial content, which has been pivotal in steering its global appeal.

The editorial direction and cover design has slowly been refined throughout its first nine issues, from an early focus on food and lifestyle. Early design refinements saw the reduction of design decoration, such as a hairline border around the centrally placed logo, to an emphasis on a simple white border cover grid system that frames feature photography.

Issue 9 saw the removal of hairlines between the title letters; it also signalled *Cereal*'s development as a style brand and the release of a new 20-page literary supplement called *Weekend*.

Publisher Rosa Park of Cereal Ltd
Creative Direction & Design Rich Stapleton
Editor Rosa Park
Photography Samantha Goh, Kate Holstein, Rich Stapleton, Anders Schonneman
Production Taylor Brothers, Hampton
Origin UK

NON-FORMAT
SEFTEL

Seftel is the title of the first album by the band of the same name. The band, formed by video director Larry Seftel, is known for its dryly humorous lyrics and the sparseness of the music. To encapsulate this sparseness, Non-Format, the long-standing creative directors for London-based Lo Recordings, collaborated with Gothenburg-based artist Ekta to create the cover art. As Jon Forss, creative partner at Non-Format, explains, 'Our overall feeling was one of a slight detachment from the subject matter, as though we're hearing an account of life observed from the seclusion of a two-way mirror. There was something about Ekta's series of painted portraits, with their featureless faces, simplicity of form and variety of colours, that seemed to fit well with this sense of distanced observation.'

Non-Format's decision to keep the title off the front of the album cover was quite deliberate and is something the studio are known for. 'We've always liked the idea of music packaging that has a nice uninterrupted image, especially as it can be quite easily shrink-wrapped and stickered with the title if needs be. That's not to say we don't like typography on our packaging and, in the case of this album, we created a custom-made typeface especially for the project.'

Ekta's paintings, originally from a 24-painting series called 'Community Series II', were a way for the artist to remove himself from a figurative painting style.

'I wanted to reduce my work as much as possible and heads or busts seemed like a good way to start. I guess I wanted my work to be less obvious and I wanted to see how much I could reduce and still be expressive, as the shapes and contours became more and more vague, colour became really important and sometimes symbolic.'

Publisher Lo Recordings
Art Direction & Design
Kjell Ekhorn & Jon Forss (Non-Format)
Illustration Ekta
Origin UK

SIMON RENAUD & JÉRÉMIE NUEL
CENTRE NATIONAL DES ARTS PLASTIQUES

Le Défi du soleil and *L'Heure de tous et consigne à vie* are the first in a collection of books accompanying contemporary artistic works exhibited in the public space at the Centre national des arts plastiques (CNAP) in Paris. The books will feature all the art, both physical and digital, exhibited in the space and the cover design will follow the same reduced grid structure with no imagery. These publications aim to trace the history of the project from the initial stages to installation.

A grid is designed to try to organize and place the typographic elements while bringing two concepts: physical space and virtual space.

The way the typography is used helps to standardize the books. Only the colour of the paper edges and the alternating typography prefaces on the grid allow each volume in the collection to be identified.

Publisher Centre national des arts plastiques (CNAP)
Art Direction (Le Défi du soleil) Simon Renaud & Jérémie Nuel
Art Direction (L'Heure de tous et consigne à vie) Simon Renaud
Design Simon Renaud
Production Snel
Origin France

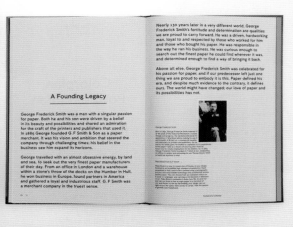

MADE THOUGHT
G . F SMITH

G . F Smith are an independent UK paper manufacturer founded in 1885. They worked with Made Thought, a London-based creative agency renowned for their classic approach to graphic design, on their rebrand, which reflected their legacy, stature and ambition.

The new simplified design direction was accompanied by the creation of an original humanist sans typeface that proudly sets the name 'G . F Smith' above '1885 onwards', a nod to the heritage of the company. The new visual identity emphasizes two new marks: a mark of custodianship and a mark that acknowledges the craft that lies behind their services and the people at the heart of the company.

The brand name on the stationery is printed using a raised gloss foil and is designed to be as simple and pared-back as possible, allowing the paper stock and print finishes to be fully appreciated. Made Thought produced a 96-page book, *Portrait of a Company*, which is a detailed history told through archive material and interviews. Printed onto 18 G . F Smith papers, it features specially commissioned portrait photography that captures a cross section of the characters who help to define the company.

Art Direction & Design Made Thought
Photography Toby Coulson
Production Push Print, Benwells;
R Young Printers
Origin UK

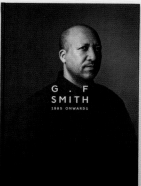

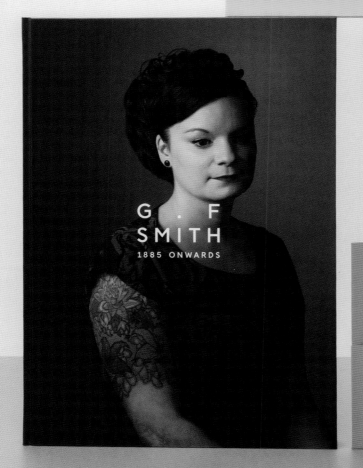

STUDIO NEWWORK
STOCK

New York-based Stock offers a global perspective on men's style by curating a mix of international menswear and beautifully crafted products. When they required a brand identity system and store packaging they assigned Studio Newwork, also based in New York, to create a logotype which was custom designed in a bold sans-serif typeface with unique trimming of the letters T and K, and a geometric letter O which is a perfect circle.

As Ryotatsu Tanaka, a partner at Studio Newwork, explains, 'The owners of Stock didn't want customers to be distracted by aggressive sales talk or unnecessary services. They let customers enjoy shopping, and they help customers professionally only when they need assistance.'

As Tanaka continues, 'The hardest thing about branding is consistency. Maintaining consistency reinforces the brand's character in the minds of customers, but lack of consistency can lead to the brand being perceived as unprofessional and unreliable. When it comes to branding for retail shopping businesses, it's crucial. The use of a black frame line is one of the consistent design elements in Stock's branding system. For packaging design and print design, all the black frame lines are the same thickness and distance from edges.'

Art Direction & Design Ryotatsu Tanaka, Ryo Kumazaki, Hitomi Ishigaki (Studio Newwork)
Origin Japan and USA

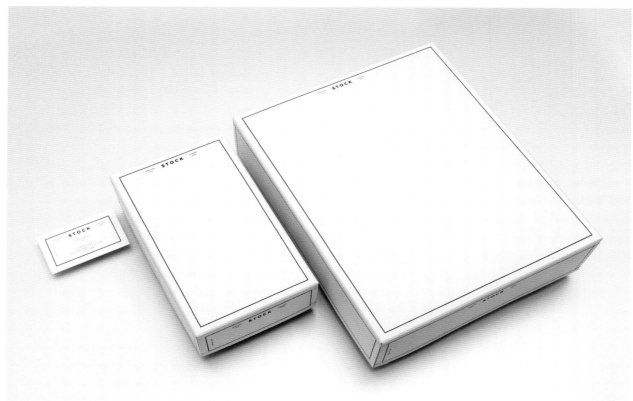

ENA CARDENAL DE LA NUEZ
PERVERSE PAINTINGS

Often ironically irreverent and equally intelligent, Albert Oehlen's work shifts between abstraction and figurative art. It is characterized by a very particular use of colour and a relentless mix of media (collages, oils, drawings) that produces a type of painting in which the accumulation of layers makes the background almost invisible. The result is disturbing, hence the title of this publication, *Perverse Paintings*, which collects paintings and drawings made in the 1990s.

To design the book, the publishers La Casa Encendida commissioned Ena Cardenal de la Nuez, a Spanish book designer renowned for her pared-down graphic approach centred around self-censorship and the removal of elements that may be too decorative or distracting. She keeps only what really matters: the cover design features a partly obscured figure-drawing covered by a chrome, with the title and the artist's name glued to the front. As Nuez explains, 'This abstraction prevents the viewer from seeing the work in its entirety; we can only guess. By doing this it turns into something mysterious, disturbing, much more perverse than it really is. And, as in the work of Oehlen, one feels that what it projects is surely much less terrible than its intention.'

Publisher La Casa Encendida, Alicia Chillida, Patronato de la Alhambra y Generalife
Art Direction & Design Ena Cardenal de la Nuez
Production TF Artes Gráficas, Cromotex
Origin Spain

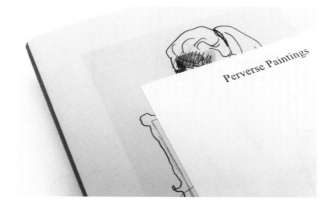

GEOMETRY GLOBAL, FRANKFURT
LEICA

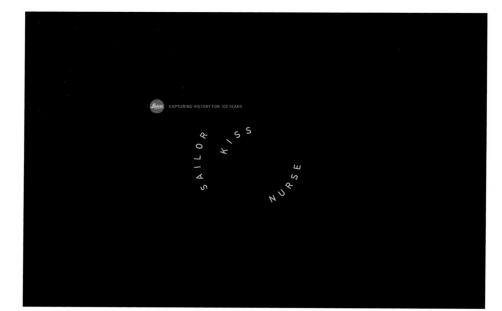

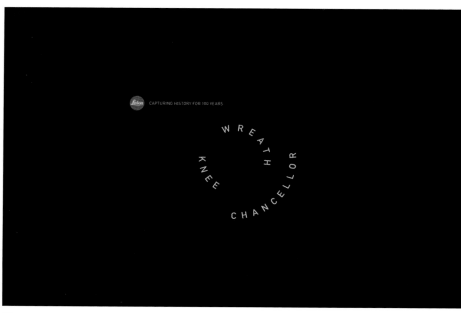

The 'Iconic Leica Pictures' print advertising campaign was conceived to celebrate the 100th anniversary of the German optics company and manufacturer of Leica cameras.

The simplified typographic posters, created by marketing agency Geometry Global, celebrate iconic Leica photography without actually showing it. Three-word sequences, arranged to mimic the functionality of a camera, are all that is needed to trigger the visual memory and align Leica with some of the most famous moments captured in small-frame photography.

Publisher Leica Camera AG
Chief Creative Officer Christian Mommertz
Deputy Managing Director Maik Hofmann
Creative Director Branding & Design Felix Dürichen
Creative Director Anita Stoll
Associate Creative Director Jutta Häussler
Senior Art Directors Oliver Rapp, Sabine Brinkmann
Senior Copywriter Philipp von Buttlar
Art Directors Nina Grün, Sabine Bartels, Mona Pust
Account Manager Tim Eisenhauer
Origin Germany

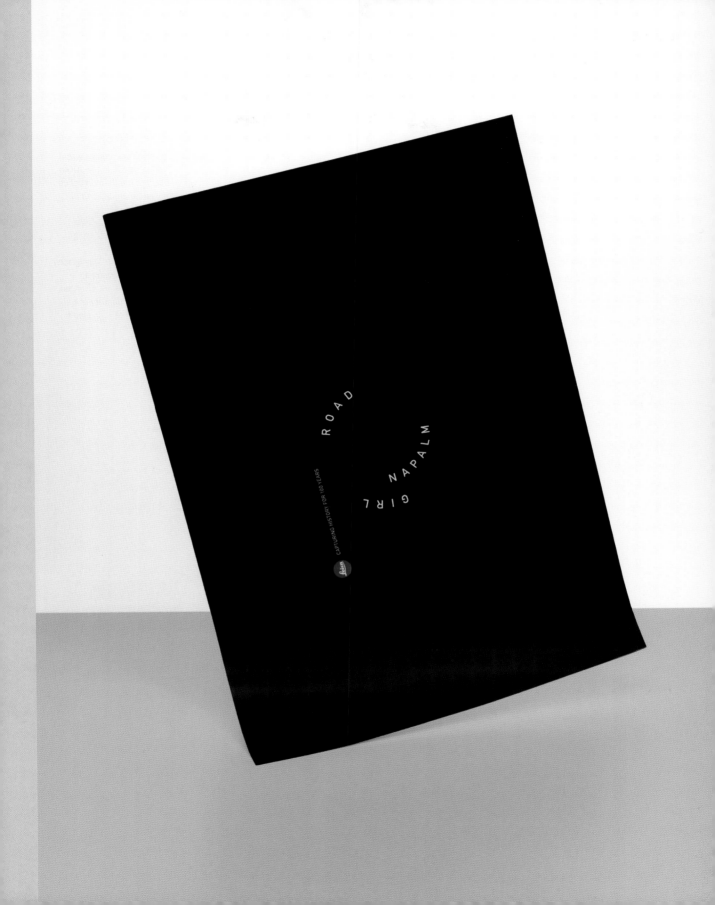

ROAD

NAPALM

GIRL

CAPTURING HISTORY FOR 100 YEARS

LOTTA NIEMINEN
PAINTBOX

Paintbox are a modern manicure studio in SoHo, New York, offering a curated selection of nail art and classic manicures. They wanted to create a brand design that reflected their attention to detail and their curated nail art designs, so they commissioned illustrator, graphic designer and art director Lotta Nieminen. She was born in Helsinki, Finland, but lives in New York.

The simple frame brand design places the nail art at the centre of focus. As Nieminen explains,

'The approach to the logo was quite straightforward – a frame, hinting at the showcase/art piece aspect of nail art, all the while doubling as a box, a nod to the name of the company. While in the form of a square, the words still manage to maintain a high level of legibility, the letters rotating in a clockwise order.'

Publisher Eleanor Langston, Brad Langston
Art Direction & Design Lotta Nieminen
Photography Jamie Nelson, Daniel Shea
Production Press New York, Bestype, Talas
Origin USA

D8 & NOMA BAR
GREENPEACE

D8, a Glasgow-based strategic design and branding agency, created Greenpeace UK's 'Our Net Gain' campaign to combat harmful industrial-scale fishing and support small-scale fishermen. D8 wanted to tackle this complex issue with one core concept in a powerful way and approached artist Noma Bar, whose work is recognized for its minimalist style of communicating multi-dimensional messages.

Bar's illustration formed the backbone of a cross-channel campaign that inspired 75,000 people to take action and lobby their local politicians, helping to turn a spotlight on the issue in the runup to the British general election in 2015. The campaign messaging was complicated, involving multiple Greenpeace stakeholders and departments, all with different interests that each had to be communicated clearly in their own right without diminishing the overall message. Bar's style was identified as an effective solution and the end product was an iconic master visual of the campaign.

Art Direction & Design D8
Illustration Noma Bar
Origin UK

Verso are a Swedish skincare company launched in 2013. They commissioned The Studio, a branding agency based in Stockholm, to create a premium unisex packaging design that would appeal to modern, design-conscious men and women. The Verso name was inspired by products that promise to 'help reverse the signs of ageing'. In Latin, 'verso' means 'reverse'. The Studio came up with the name, which became the central concept for the brand, and developed the range of pared-down, black-and-white typographic-based packaging.

The 'reverse' idea is further illustrated on the packaging through the large numerals which are set in reverse (i.e. mirrored). The numbers differentiate the products and suggest the order of use within the series.

The packaging was produced by Göteborgstryckeriet, with the paper and printing techniques developed in collaboration with The Studio. The outer packaging is a fine German watercolour paper which is hot-foil stamped. Using sharp-edged corners and off-white colour in contrast to the glossy black foil, the packaging has a premium tactile quality with a clean, classic and timeless finish. Aside from adding shelf-appeal, the goal with the packaging was to create a product that people would leave out on the bathroom counter.

Art Direction Susanna Nygren Barrett
Design Tom Miller, Torbjörn Kilhberg, Henrik Karlsson (The Studio)
Strategic Project Manager Mattias Börjesson
Production Göteborgstryckeriet
Origin Sweden

VERSO
DARK SPOT FIX
WITH RETINOL 8

VERSO
SUPER EYE SERUM
WITH RETINOL 8

VERSO
SUPER FACIAL SERUM
WITH RETINOL 8

VERSO
NIGHT CREAM
WITH RETINOL 8

VERSO
DAY CREAM
WITH RETINOL 8

VERSO
FOAMING CLEANSER
FOR DAILY USE

ARTIVA DESIGN
PLUG-IN

The exhibition *Plug-In 2013–2003*, a ten-year overview of the collaboration with Plug-In publishing, was shown at the Museo d'Arte Contemporanea di Villa Croce in Genoa, Italy. Italian design studio Artiva set up the exhibition with Emanuele Piccardo (the editor-in-chief). Renowned for their minimal black-and-white work, Artiva designed the brochure and accompanying poster. The resulting typographic title design runs over four pages, giving a sense of continuity. As Daniele De Batté, design partner at Artiva, explains, 'Our work stands out for a peculiar balance in shapes. I align myself with John Pawson's ideas on minimalism. It's the essence of life, the absence of the superfluous, like in Japanese Zen methodology or Thoreau's search for simplicity.'

Publisher Plug-In
Art Direction & Design
Daniele De Batté, Davide Sossi
(Artiva Design)
Origin Italy

LES GRAPHIQUANTS
GIL RIGOULET – MOLITOR – ÉTÉ 1985

The Molitor swimming pool opened in 1929 in the 16th district of Paris. It has always been a cherished architectural icon and has had several uses: as a post-war public swimming pool, a street-art squat in the late 1980s and a high-end hotel in 2014.

Gil Rigoulet, a French photographer, was fascinated by the Art Deco architecture of the building and its atmosphere, and was often seen roaming the alleys of the pool in the mid-1980s. (M) Editions, a French publishing house, has re-released Rigoulet's iconic black-and-white photographs as a limited edition book in a handmade box that comes with 15 silver prints and a map of the pool, which shows where each shot was taken.

The book's cover is a mathematical narrative composition with five lines and 25 dots, placed symmetrically between the five lines. It elegantly replicates the architecture of the swimming pool.

Publisher (M) Editions
Art Direction Marie Sepchat, Gil Rigoulet, Les Graphiquants
Design Les Graphiquants
Production Maestro Edition
Origin France

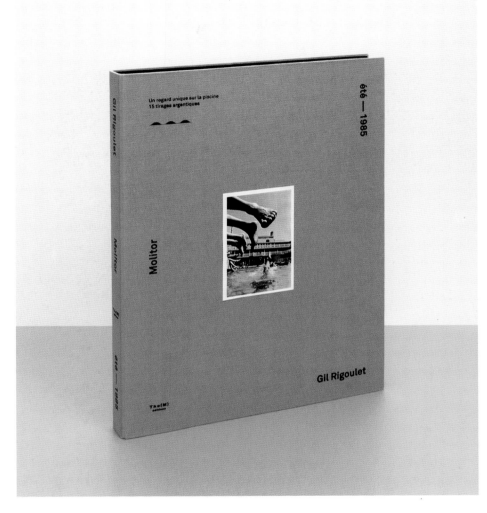

SHAZ MADANI
RIPOSTE

Riposte is a London-based independent magazine for women. Each issue follows the same editorial direction with five ideas, four meetings, three features, two essays and one icon. The magazine features profiles of bold, interesting women, who speak openly and honestly about their experiences and opinions. The interviews often feature candid responses, discussing individual successes, failures, work, passions and perspectives.

The design direction of the first five issues, featuring a type-only cover with a portrait photograph on the back, is the same for each issue. As Shaz Madani, the art director, explains, 'The type-only cover reflects our desire to make sure the women featured are not judged or represented by just their looks, but instead celebrated for their ideas and achievements. It was a purposeful departure from the image-obsessed magazine world. So its minimal design is more functional than aesthetic, but has become an important part of our visual identity.'

Stylistic interventions and typographic tricks are kept to a minimum and instead the focus is on creating beautiful and simple spreads that don't overshadow the content, allowing the images and words the space to breath.

Publisher Danielle Pender
Art Direction & Design Shaz Madani
Editor Danielle Pender
Photography Nick Ballon, Jiro Schneider, Francesca Jane Allen
Production CPI
Origin UK

Riposte

A Smart Magazine for Women
Issue 3

Nº3

In this issue:
Anna Trevelyan,
Nathalie
Du Pasquier,
Samantha Urbani,
and Victoria Siddall.

UK 10 EU 11 US 16

THE ENTENTE
COLOPHON FOUNDRY

The Colophon's 'five years' catalogue celebrates the creation of 26 typefaces made between 2009 and 2014 by Colophon Foundry. The catalogue showcases the fonts designed by Anthony Burrill, Benjamin Critton, Alison Haigh, Oscar & Ewan, StudioMakgill, The Entente and Dries Wiewauters.

The Swiss-bound A4 publication on uncoated paper was released in an edition of 300. It was stripped of any branding and only features five small dots to signify each of the five years.

The typefaces are showcased on multiple paper stocks printed on a single-sided board that features each of the 26 compositions made on behalf of each of the typefaces. An essay by Aileen Kwun of Project Projects and Superscript introduces the book and provides information on each typeface and its provenance.

To celebrate the launch of the publication, an exhibition was held at the KK Outlet in London, featuring original artworks that used and abused each of the 26 typefaces.

Art Direction & Design Anthony Sheret, Edd Harrington, Benjamin Critton (Colophon Foundry/The Entente)
Production Generation Press
Origin UK

CARL NAS ASSOCIATES
TANGENT GC

Tangent GC is an eco-friendly garment and shoe care product range from Sweden. The company's motto, 'Wear your favourites for longer', is reflected in their identity and packaging which has a timeless numerical design system. Each product is assigned its own ascending number upon release. There is minimal use of typographic weights and sizes, which are executed on neutral colours and materials.

The Tangent GC product range has a deliberately simple black-and-white label designed to blend in with the interiors of the fashion stores and high-end interior design shops where the product is sold. The neutral tones also help highlight the natural wood, metallics and glass materials used in the packaging.

Art Direction & Design
Carl Nas (Carl Nas Associates)
Origin Sweden

DESIGNBOLAGET
NATIONAL GALLERY OF DENMARK

What is the X room? The National Gallery of Denmark has created x-rummet, an experimental space for contemporary art that will showcase six artists over three years. It exhibits artwork that reflects on and challenges how museum spaces function.

For this venture, the gallery asked Designbolaget, a Copenhagen-based design studio, to create a visual identity. Claus Due, the founder of the studio, observed, 'focusing on the X as a marker for a space, we created an X out of two lines, one line representing the institution, the other being the artist. The "institution's" line is a constant, while the line representing the artist changes from one exhibition to the next.'

This graphic solution signifies the 'break this experimental space makes with the traditional way of presenting art, as well as giving us clean graphic shapes to play around with. The simplicity of the design makes it easy to adapt to different medias – print and moving images.'

The strength of the bold X is that it stands on its own – whether on the exhibition catalogues or covering a large expanse for exhibition signage. The catalogues are printed on inexpensive paper and stapled together for an unpretentious look.

Publisher National Gallery of Denmark
Art Direction Claus Due (Designbolaget)
Design Claus Due, Johanne Lian Olsen
Production Narayana Press
Origin Denmark

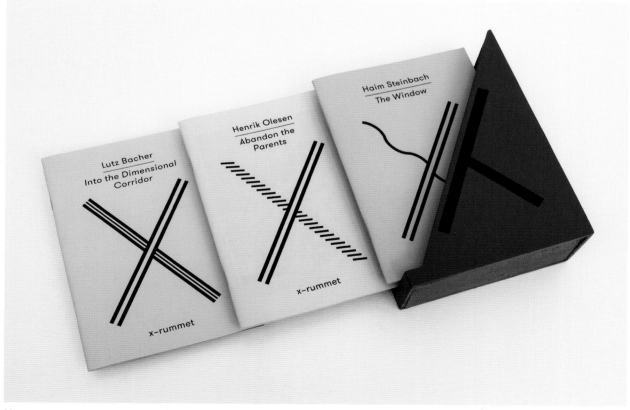

UMA/DESIGN FARM
INSTITUTE OF DISASTER MITIGATION
FOR URBAN CULTURAL HERITAGE

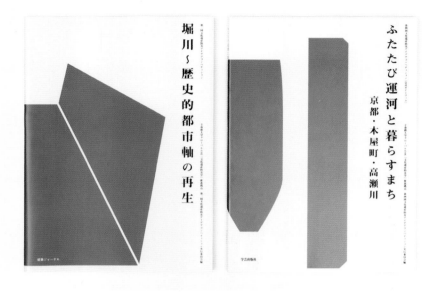

UMA/Design Farm is a design studio founded by art director and designer Yuma Harada and is based in Osaka. The studio creates pared-back typographic and geometric design solutions for cultural and lifestyle clients.

Each year, the Institute of Disaster Mitigation for Urban Cultural Heritage at Ritsumeikan University, Japan, holds an annual 'Ideas Competition' to appeal for ways to safeguard traditional temples, shrines and streets from demolition at the hands of disaster and advancing modern technology.

The most innovative results are published in *Ideas Competition for Strategy on Disaster Mitigation of Cultural Heritage and Historic Cities*, a book that summarizes the importance of preserving traditional buildings for future generations.

The minimalist, geometric shapes on the front covers represent the intended sites for preservation. For each issue, the shape is rendered in a different metallic spot colour.

Publisher 1–3: Kenchiku Journal,
4: Gakugei Shuppansha
Art Direction Yuma Harada
(UMA/Design Farm)
Design Keisuke Yamazoe
(UMA/Design Farm)
Production Daishinsha Inc.
Origin Japan

Page 1: Great Expectations and *Golden Meaning* are graphic-design-inspired books published by London-based GraphicDesign&. *Page 1: Great Expectations* is a collection of the work of 70 graphic designers and *Golden Meaning* of 55 designers. They visually explore the first page of *Great Expectations* by Charles Dickens and the 'divine proportion', the golden mean, respectively.

The books are the first two in the GraphicDesign& series. Art director and designer Lucienne Roberts explains, '*Golden Meaning* includes all manner of representations and explorations of the golden mean so its cover design is straightforward and simple. It shows the golden ratio, 1: 1.618, set in the font Graphik.

To emphasize the binary nature of this ratio, the two figure 1s and the colon and decimal point align. The use of the ellipsis, in "infinity foil", makes clear that this number has no end... The *Page 1: Great Expectations* cover shows a series of apparently randomly placed tabs of fluorescent colour. They are, however, scaled and arranged very precisely. Each block matches one of the 70 folios on the layouts inside. This makes the cover an abstracted version of all the page 1s within.'

Publisher GraphicDesign&
Art Direction & Design LucienneRoberts+
Production CPI Mackays, Lecturis
Origin UK

MOUSEGRAPHICS
HARMONIAN

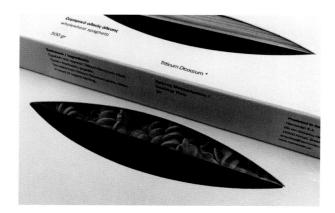

Harmonian are a high-quality food production company based in Athens, Greece. They encourage casual gourmands to 'regain health' through the use of their pure, unprocessed, organic foods.

When he commissioned the packaging design, Georgios Stournaras, CEO of Harmonian, wanted to reflect the company's healthy and environmentally conscious standpoint. He approached Athens-based Mousegraphics to create a design 'that has an aura of exclusivity, which should be rooted in elegance and measured values to convey radical simplicity.'

The packaging design needed a unified visual statement which would work across Harmonian's extensive range of natural products, including olive oil, flour, pasta, herb infusions and fleur de sel. A simplified graphic approach inspired by the triticum dicoccum variety of wheat seeds, one of the earliest domesticated dual-core crops in the ancient world, was adopted to convey harmony and balance, enhancing the mathematical perfection of the spindle shape.

The shape was partially die-cut into the front of the pasta packaging. This approach was inspired by the Italian artist Lucio Fontana's 'taglis', the slashed-canvas artworks *Spatial Concept, Waiting*, which were created between 1958 and 1968.

To enhance the natural feel of the product range, a special ink was developed for the packaging graphics; it imitated a silk-screen effect.

Recycled materials were chosen whenever possible throughout the range to lessen the environmental impact. Glass tubes with cork caps were preferred for their practicality and reusability, and their preservation qualities, while more conservative tin bottles were also used as they are the easiest material to recycle.

Art Direction Greg Tsaknakis, Joshua Olsthoorn (Mousegraphics)
Design Joshua Olsthoorn
Illustration Ioanna Papaioannou
Origin Greece

NICOLE ARNETT PHILLIPS
TYPOGRAPH.JOURNAL VOL. 1

This debut volume of *Typograph. Journal* was originally published in an edition of 1,000 by typographic specialist Nicole Arnett Phillips, who lives in Brisbane, Australia. It contains visual research, ideation, interviews and a series of tools to encourage creative confidence and continued learning.

As a reflection of contemporary culture, the volume is set out so it reads like a series of sound-bites. Each two-page spread contains 'an idea, an inspiration, a catalyst or a resource' that can be read alone or as a thread to form part of the curated collection of themes and ideas. Volume 1 poses the question 'Can a text be readerly and experimental?' It is visually referenced by a cutaway lowercase 'a' on the cover. As Phillips puts it, 'I am very interested in exploring how much we can distort, subtract or manipulate letterforms before they lose their meaning. So for this cover I wanted to test how far we can reduce an archetype before it became abstract – to highlight the tension between form and function in typography.'

The self-published journal is burst-bound and printed on Grange paper stock from K. W. Doggett. Phillips continues, 'It was really important to me that the document was printed on Australian paper stock (of which there are not many options left I am afraid – most mills have closed down and the same is true of print-finishing businesses). But the product is as local as I could make it.'

Publisher Nicole Arnett Phillips
Art Direction & Design Nicole Arnett Phillips
Production Nicole Arnett Phillips, Foyer Printing
Origin Australia

RITXI OSTÁRIZ
TODMORDEN 513

This monochromatic series of posters was created to promote *Todmorden 513 (Concerto for Orchestra)* by Markus Reuter, a German composer and musician. It was recorded live in 2014 with Thomas A. Blomster directing and the Colorado Chamber Orchestra playing. Reuter describes how the piece attempts to create 'a new sound world'. Todmorden is a small market town in Yorkshire in the UK, but in German the word 'tod' means 'death' and 'morden' means 'to murder'. For Reuter, 'it's part of my understanding of the world that the impression that something gives you is not necessarily what it is, or means. Especially if you're speaking different languages.'

Basque designer Ritxi Ostáriz explains the ideas behind

his own graphic response: 'it represents a sophisticated extraterrestrial civilization sending communication signals that the human race receives but cannot understand. Stanley Kubrick's *2001. A Space Odyssey* and Carl Sagan's *Contact* are the main conceptual influences for the visuals. Starting from a high-resolution photograph of an asteroid, all the compositions were created by distorting it with different values. And these values are related to the musical composition, so every shape includes a hidden message inside.'

Publisher Colorado Chamber Orchestra
Art Direction & Design Ritxi Ostáriz
Origin Spain, Germany

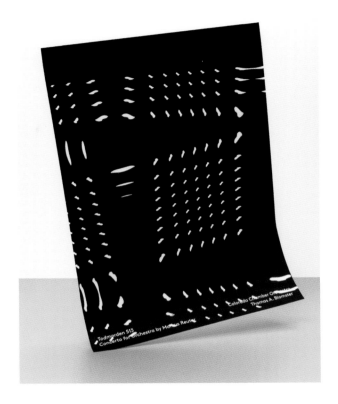

JOHN MORGAN STUDIO
ARTREVIEW

John Morgan Studio are a London-based practice working with contemporary arts institutes and publishers. The studio's design output is underpinned by a carefully considered, reduced aesthetic that has been recognized by the Design Museum, London's 'Design of the Year' award on three occasions.

In September 2013 the studio were appointed art directors of *ArtReview*, one of the world's leading contemporary art magazines. Their minimal cover template redesign is immediately recognizable and places the issue's theme at the bottom of each cover. This approach is consistent throughout the nine issues published each year, including the 'Power 100' special, a guide to the personalities driving the global arts scene, and 'Future Greats', which identifies the artists to watch in the coming year.

The 2014 edition of 'Future Greats', with commissioned cover artwork by photographers Luke & Nik, features striking, reduced, white-out portraits to create a minimalistic cover design that is a stark contrast to the majority of cluttered newsstand titles.

The 2014 edition of 'Power 100' is entirely blank, signalling a radical departure from previous issues, where artists have been commissioned to create an original artwork. Mysteriously, that year's cover art, created by Paul Chan, was deemed too offensive by the magazine. Although John Morgan proposed 'putting the magazine in a bag or covering the image with a sticker', the work remains entirely invisible, not even appearing inside the issue.

Publisher ArtReview
Art Direction John Morgan Studio
Photography Luke & Nik
Origin UK

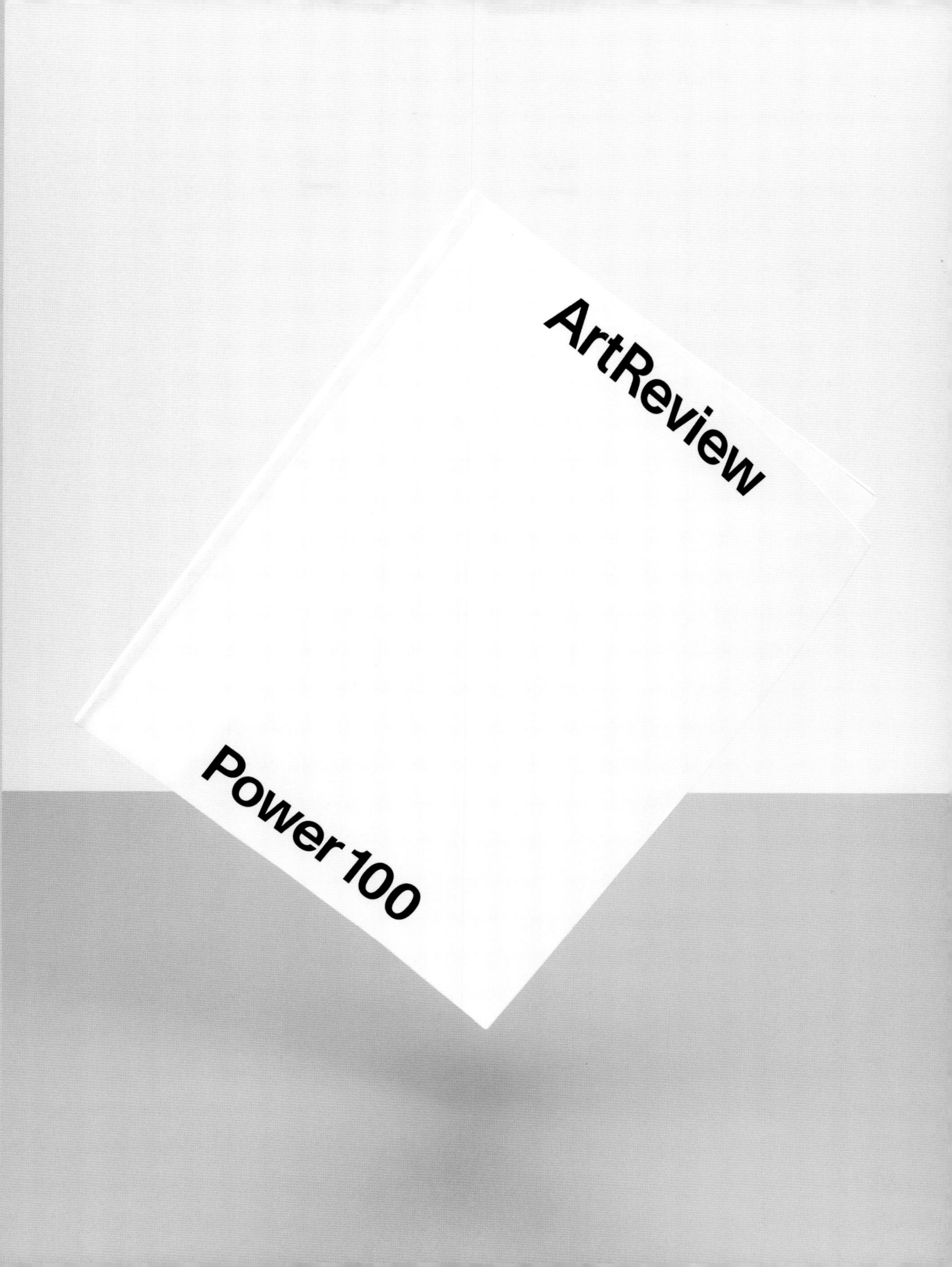

ArtReview

Power 100

STOCKHOLM DESIGN LAB
ASKUL

In their own words, the Japanese company 'keeps Japan stocked with everything it needs to work, from paper, pens and batteries to bags, chairs, tools, coffee and noodles. Askul has everything.'

In 2005 Askul were looking for something new, wanting to establish a clear, compelling visual identity for their own-brand products. With the shared Japanese and Swedish design values of simplicity, clarity and economy in mind, and the benefit of a fresh set of eyes from outside Japan, Askul asked Stockholm Design Lab (SDL) to reimagine their brand identity.

Björn Kusoffsky, CEO and co-founder of SDL, explains, 'we introduced a system of packaging and product design that, in the context of the typical Askul catalogue, was striking in its calm, stylish simplicity. Each item was reduced to its bare essentials: form and essential information. In Japan, batteries are categorized using numerals, 1–4. The simple, straightforward design highlights this important piece of product information while sweeping away all irrelevant detail.' The batteries are also colour-coded as a further aid to identification.

Askul think 'this most mundane of products has become something new and fun – desirable, even, and there have been more than 230 million battery sales since SDL got involved.'

Art Direction & Design Stockholm Design Lab
Production Askul
Origin Japan

ANYMADE STUDIO
7TH NEW ZLIN SALON

The 7th New Zlin Salon, a contemporary art exhibition, is held every three years at the Regional Gallery of Fine Arts in Zlin, the Czech Republic. It is inspired by traditional Zlin salons, which were organized by the Bata company between 1936 and 1948 to display contemporary Czech fine art and showcase the connection between business and culture. The reincarnation of the exhibition takes place in Bata's old factory halls and represents the work of more than 90 contemporary Czech and Slovak artists.

The exhibition catalogue features bold geometric shapes, which emphasize the tradition associated with the exhibition. As Petr Cabalka, design partner at Anymade Studio, explains, 'The geometric cover design was inspired by Zlin functionalist architecture from the 1930s. We designed a range of visual communications that reflects the wide range of art featured (paintings, sculptures, photography and installations) in the book and wanted to keep a consistent graphic layout to be applied on all applications.'

Bold sans serif typography was applied to the cover design to create a contemporary interpretation. Cabalka continues, 'we applied a strong typeface with characteristic letters. We love the Colophon Foundry and we often use their typefaces.'

Publisher Regional Gallery of Fine Arts, Zlin
Art Direction & Design Petr Cabalka, Filip Nerad (Anymade Studio)
Production Tiskárna Helbich, a.s.
Origin The Czech Republic

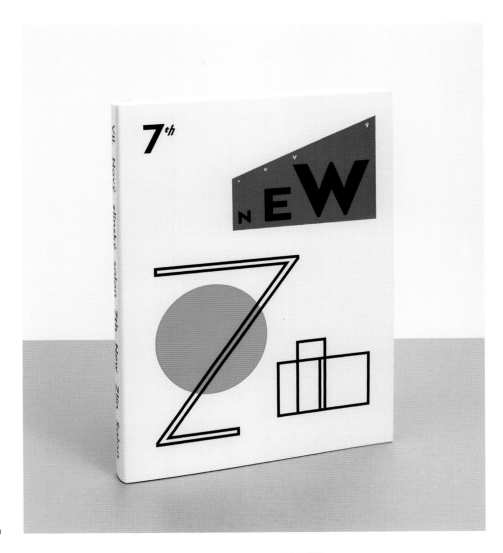

FONS HICKMANN M23
AMNESTY INTERNATIONAL

Fons Hickmann M23 are a
Berlin-based graphic design
studio founded by art director
Fons Hickmann. The studio have
a long-term relationship with
Amnesty International, the human
rights charity, creating striking
and simple visuals to convey
campaign messages. The studio's
graphic language is based on a
straightforward and very clear
typographic system animated
by very strong illustrations and
graphics that enable instant
comprehension of the information.
As Hickmann explains, 'The
content is dramatized. Being
a highly visual medium, like
a system of signals, the use of a
very hard character for headlines
and graphics, contrasts between
colours, and variations of very
graphic pictograms, by way
of illustration, means a highly
pertinent manifest tone emanates
from these choices.'

The series of bold, graphic
posters, accompanied by the
newsprint magazine *Amnesty
Aktion*, delivers a strong message,
using a minimalist aesthetic.

Art Direction Fons Hickmann M23
Origin Germany

PUTIN
WE ARE WATCHING YOU!
AMNESTY INTERNATIONAL
WWW.AMNESTY.DE/RUSSLAND

BRH+
LAGO

LAGO are an Italian furniture design company who created the 36e8 modular system based on the square, which means consumers can create their own interiors by assembling a simple 36.8 x 36.8 cm-square module.

The 36e8 book was published to showcase the infinite variety of settings and compositions that the square module system allows. Printed in one colour, black, with bright yellow title type set using Kurz hot-stamping technology, the cover is a celebration of self-assembly. As Marco Rainò of BRH+, an Italian graphic design studio, explains, 'Geometric forms represent the 36e8 modules – that are not yet touched by the pictured hands – embossed to underline potential for the user to create their own "interior life".'

The book design was conceived to enhance the distinctive characteristic of LAGO, which is linear, rigorous and deeply contemporary. The sequence of pages is organized to create a story through the conjunction of graphic design elements with evocative images.

Art Direction Barbara Brondi, Marco Rainò
Design BRH+
Photography Delfino Sisto Legnani, Stefano Aiti
Styling BRH+, Make That Studio
Production Grafiche Antiga
Origin Italy

BARNES & WEBB
LONDON POSTCODE HONEY

London Postcode Honey, created by the beehive rental company Barnes & Webb, is a range of raw honey produced and harvested by hand in London.

The bold black-and-white label design, reminiscent of the black type on white backgrounds used on London street signage, highlights the London postal area where the beehives are kept and where the honey is created.

The black-and-white approach allows for the colour of the honey to shine. It has a slightly different hue depending on the nectar available in that specific postal area. As Chris Barnes, creative partner at Barnes & Webb, puts it, 'Printing a small label in black and white felt the most balanced solution. It was also the most cost effective for our limited budget. We wanted to have gold leaf in there too but we couldn't afford it!'

Art Direction Chris Barnes,
Paul Webb (Barnes & Webb)
Design Chris Barnes
Production Barnes & Webb
Origin UK

PASCAL ALEXANDER
CLUB ZUKUNFT

Club Zukunft is an electronic music club in the centre of Zurich in Switzerland. Their posters take a bold, minimalist typographic approach to advertising the club's monthly programme.

Pascal Alexander, the art director for Club Zukunft, has created a striking series of promotional posters, usually only printed in an edition of two, which are located in the club's entry hall. He uses white typography on a black background: an approach centred around his preference for plainness.

Alexander explains, 'I do them only for a few selected events and they're the only advertising alongside a monthly program which, too, is only available at the club.'

His stark posters work as a statement from the club. 'The best club is an empty space with nothing but a sound system and some lights, providing a blank canvas for the music.'

Publisher Club Zukunft
Art Direction & Design Pascal Alexander
Production Kurt Scheuble
(Siebdruckmanufaktur)
Origin Switzerland

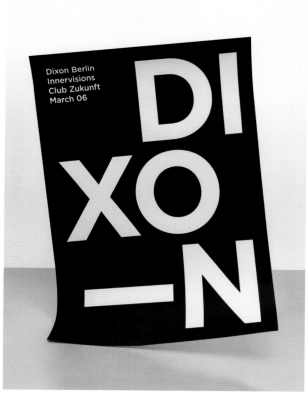

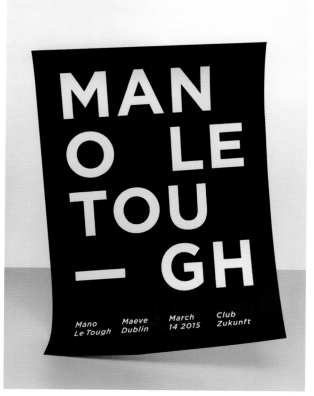

ROMANFLUEGEL

RO
MA
NF
LUE
GEL

ROMAN
FLUEGEL

DIAL REC
PLAYHOUSE

ALEX
DALLAS

FATHER
& SON

FEBRUARY
27 2015

CLUB
ZUKUNFT

DIENER 33
ZURICH

DALSTON CREATIVE
ÅKESTAM HOLST

Based in Stockholm, Sweden, Åkestam Holst are an advertising agency with clients such as Swebus, SAS and Audi. To celebrate the agency's most iconic projects over the last 15 years, Swedish publishing house Arvinius + Orfeus published a monograph showcasing their philosophy through a series of sections detailing their work. Intended to be read and not just flicked through, the book is designed to have a naive, personal feeling, which is how Åkestam Holst see themselves.

The typographic cover uses letters from the agency's name connected by a series of hairlines. As Magnus Darke, creative partner at Stockholm-based Dalston Creative, who are art directors on the project, says 'The typographic solution is meant to symbolize the turbulent but interesting journey that the agency has been through over the years. There have been many detours and different paths to follow and with the letters we are mimicking that the journey has not been a straight one.'

Author Carin Fredlund
Publisher Arvinius + Orfeus Publishing
Art Direction Magnus Darke, Sofia Darke (Dalston Creative)
Photography Åkestam Holst, Daniel Blom
Production Livonia Printers
Origin Sweden

STUDIO HAUSHERR
TALENT

Talent is a range of soft drinks manufactured using only natural tea ingredients. Their belief that soft drinks are over-sweetened and contain artificial flavours is central to the product and packaging design, which was created by Studio Hausherr, a Berlin-based graphic design studio.

As Sebastian Conradi from Talent explains, 'We wanted Talent's label design to properly reflect our beverage's pure and natural flavours. Whereas many soft drinks' labels are overloaded with visual exaggerations, we chose to do the opposite and keep it simple.'

The label design is clean and simple, accented by three muted colours, very different to the packaging adopted by the majority of soft-drink manufacturers.

Art Direction & Design Sven Hausherr (Studio Hausherr)
Origin Germany

JOP VAN BENNEKOM & VERONICA DITTING
THE GENTLEWOMAN

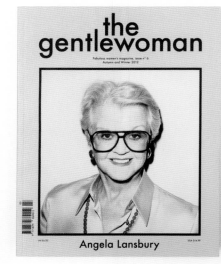

Angela Lansbury

Beyoncé

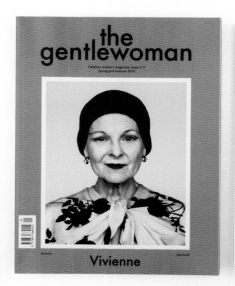

Vivienne

Björk

The spectacular sonic genius

Described as a 'fabulous women's magazine', *The Gentlewoman* celebrates modern women of style and purpose. The independent biannual magazine works with writers and photographs of the highest calibre to create an intelligent perspective on fashion, one focused on personal style, glamour, personality and warmth.

The Gentlewoman is a global success story and a beacon for contemporary magazine publishing. Each issue is instantly recognizable because of its simplified graphic direction, with few or no cover lines. In the words of Veronica Ditting, the magazine's art director, 'Our team enjoys modernist values and their association with aspirational, politicized thinking, intelligence and creative ambition. It's fair to characterize our design tastes as fairly spare and specific, though, and our photographic preferences as tending towards candid portraiture and real life – we're not particularly interested in fantasy.'

Beautiful cover portrait photography of a lead woman is central to the design philosophy and the choice of cover star is intended to be a compliment. Ditting continues, 'We love the idea of people seeing Vivienne Westwood's face on the newsstand and their requiring no further information than her Christian name to understand why she's important and beloved enough to occupy that special space on our magazine.'

Publisher Fantastic Woman Ltd
Creative Direction Jop van Bennekom
Art Direction Veronica Ditting
Editor Penny Martin
Design Assistant Jenny Hirons, Karishma Rafferty, Aude Debout, Andrew Osman
Photography Terry Richardson, Zoë Ghertner, Alasdair McLelian
Origin UK

NEIL DONNELLY
CRITIQUE OF EVERYDAY LIFE

Verso Books are a UK-based independent publisher specializing in radical books. They work exclusively with Rumors, an art direction studio, to realize the complex themes addressed in their publications. For the book *Critique of Everyday Life* by the French Marxist philosopher Henri Lefebvre, Rumors commissioned Neil Donnelly, a graphic designer based in Brooklyn, New York, to design the cover of the first omnibus edition.

The simplified design features an intriguing move away from the traditional book-cover format, utilizing the spine as the focal point for the title rather than the front. As Donnelly explains, 'The design acknowledges the book as an object by transferring all information to the spine, subtly but dramatically tweaking the quotidian form of the book.'

Publisher Verso
Art Direction Andy Pressman (Rumors)
Design Neil Donnelly
Production Maple Press
Origin USA

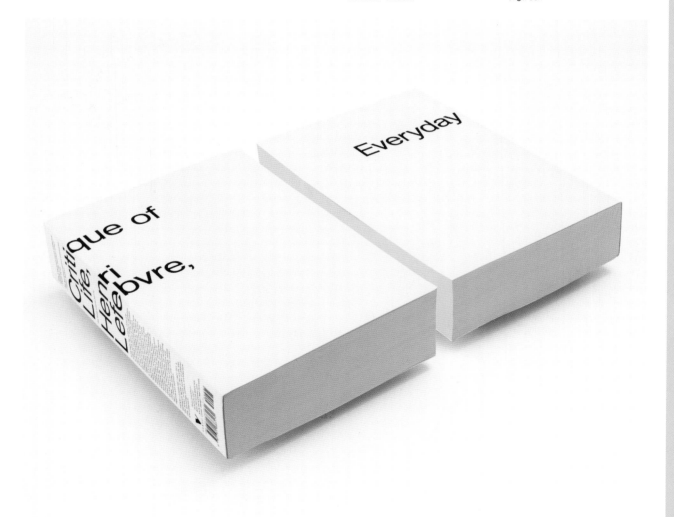

DANIEL HALSALL
GOGO PENGUIN

GoGo Penguin are a three-piece acoustic electronic band where the pianist is central to creating the melodies on the tracks. They were formed in Manchester, UK.

Daniel Halsall created the art direction for the band's second album, v2.0. He has an interest in minimalist music design and has worked with Gondwana Records since its inception in 2008. Halsall explains, 'I have always been interested in minimal design. In my early 20s, I was a big fan of The Designers Republic and Alex Rutterford, especially their work with Warp Records where they created beautifully minimal designs. I also love Reid Miles's legendary work with Blue Note Records.'

The black-and-white piano keyboard and the band's musical approach, which fuses melodic live drumming and melodies, provided Halsall with inspiration for the design. 'The black lines represent the black keys on the piano. There are 36 black keys on the piano and there are 36 black lines on the cover. GoGo's music is very tight, both rhythmically and in its structure, and the stiff straight lines reflect that. The lines also create a form that looks like it has been broken and then rearranged, which mirrors their sound, in particular on the track 'One Percent', where the band mimic the sound of a skipping CD.'

Publisher Gondwana Records, Phoenix Music International
Art Direction & Design Daniel Halsall
Production Gondwana Records
Origin UK

BOB DESIGN
NORDIC

Based in Oslo, Nordic are an architectural practice launched as a modern version of the long-established Narud Stokke Wiig Architects + Planners. The modernization process included an overhaul of the brand, which cemented their position as industry leaders within the Scandinavian market. This regional recognition was an important aspect of the rebranding, which fell to London- and Zurich-based studio BOB Design. As Mireille Burkhardt, creative director at BOB, explains, 'Nordic means "to be of or related to the north or northern lands", so we developed a new identity that centres on the north arrow. It is bold in form, reliably consistent and with a behavioural bias towards the top or "northern" edge of any space it inhabits.'

The geometric arrow device is central to the rebranding, with all other design and typographic elements aligning themselves to this central marker. Created in a visually strong black-and-white colour palette, the new branding is a combination of a map (or compass-like) arrow and a Nordic initial 'N'. The logotype reads and spreads outwards from the core arrow logo, which is directly echoed in the forms of the letters R and I. Geometric circular forms for O, D and C are introduced as a counterbalance to the hard geometric shapes. The minimalist colour scheme is complemented by Aurora Green, another regional reference celebrating the Northern Lights.

Art Direction Mireille Burkhardt, Kieran O'Connor (BOB Design)
Design Aaron Merrigan, Clara Goodger, Haider Muhdi
Origin Norway

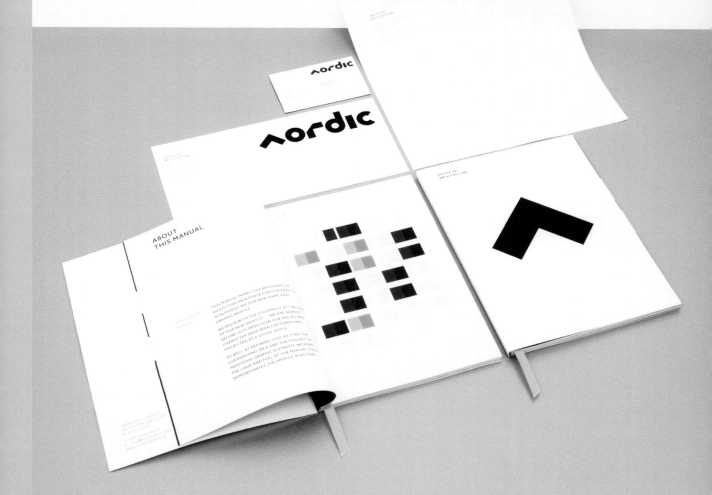

PLUS MÛRS STUDIO
GÉRARD HOLTZ

Gérard Holtz is a very well-known sports anchorman on French television. He was awarded the Ordre national du Mérite by Nicolas Sarkozy, the then French prime minister, in 2010.

As a testimony to the charismatic presenter, Plus Mûrs Studio, based in Nantes, dedicated a Tumblr site to him. It is filled with sports, style and graphic design references. As Vincent Labas from Plus Mûrs explains, 'He's like a spiritual father. We decided to compile images each year to keep an eye on aesthetic trends.'

The two-volume books are a printed version of the Tumblr site. They reference the graphic style on the site, also featuring quotations from Holtz. The simplified design, with serif typography for volume one and sans serif for volume two, was chosen to allow the imagery to speak for itself.

Art Direction & Design Plus Mûrs Studio
Origin France

HENRIK NYGREN DESIGN
SERPENTINE GALLERIES

'512 Hours' by the Serbian performance artist Marina Abramović was a conceptual art event at the Serpentine Galleries, London, in the summer of 2014. Upon arrival, visitors were invited to remove all personal belongings and wear a set of headphones, which completely blocked out the ambient noise of the gallery, leaving them free to wander around the space in self-reflection. During '512 Hours', Abramović – sometimes with a team of staff, sometimes with a set of props – interacted with visitors by inviting them to look out of windows and stand in front of walls. They became the performance art themselves.

Public reactions were recorded and displayed daily in an online visual diary, and a selection of the ambient noise created was recorded onto a vinyl record. A spoken presentation by Abramović of her life manifesto was on the reverse. Pressed onto white vinyl by the music and art publisher The Vinyl Factory, the limited-edition releases were available in an edition of 100, signed and numbered.

To visualize the open, self-reflective nature of the performance, Swedish graphic design studio Henrik Nygren Design were commissioned to create the artwork. The resulting clean, simplified design, devoid of any extraneous decoration, was presented on a white sleeve that housed the white vinyl record. Simplification is an important aspect of the studio's design work, as Nygren explains: 'Because good design, still, is as little design as possible.'

Publisher Serpentine Galleries
Art Direction Henrik Nygren Design
Design Henrik Nygren, Pernilla Forsberg
Production The Vinyl Factory
Origin UK

M35
ICEBERGS DINING ROOM AND BAR

M35 are a multi-disciplinary agency formed by creative director Jamie Mitchell. The studio were invited to rebrand Icebergs, the dining room located just off Bondi Beach in Sydney, taking inspiration from its unique location.

The design concept is centred around assimilating the dining room into its beach environment. As Mitchell explains, 'With an awe-inspiring view out over Bondi Beach, we wanted to create an invisible restaurant brand that allowed the beach location, with its continual tide movement, to come to the fore.'

Tides dictate much of the leisure activity in Bondi, and the design encapsulates this by creating a virtual tideline, which is carried through all promotional formats. The typography often sits in the background, most evidently in the business card designs, below, which feature the rising Bondi tideline gradually obstructing the logo.

Likewise, the café menu opposite indicates the varying heights of the tide at different times of the day. At lower tides, the logotype can be seen clearly. At high tide, it is completely obscured.

The colour palette and print finishing draw creative stimulus from the name 'Icebergs' itself. A transparent foil is used, creating a minimalist white-on-white design, which is complemented by a crisp aqua blue.

Art Direction M35
Origin Australia

REDUCTION

LISTER

L
S
T
R

SUNDAY JUNE 8TH
FROM 6PM
ICEBERGS BAR

10

TEN

PLATES

P
L
T
S

LIMITED FREE
PLATES

10

TEN

YEARS

Y
R
S

CHRISTOF NÜSSLI
AMOK

Amok is a personal commentary on the absurdities of the world by German photographer André Gelpke. Encapsulating the artist's motto, 'Photography is a whore, never faithful, always feigning', it explores Gelpke's mania for taking photographs and challenging the world with his pictures.

The book was designed by Zurich-based graphic designer Christof Nüssli and features a bold typographic composition screen-printed onto the thread-sewn hardcover. As Nüssli explains, 'The inside of the book consists of pictures taken only by André Gelpke. There is no single image that can feature on the cover, therefore it was very clear from the beginning that we should use a type-only cover for this photobook.'

Publisher Cpress, Spector Books
Art Direction & Design Christof Nüssli
Photography André Gelpke
Production Druckerei zu Altenburg GmbH
Origin Switzerland

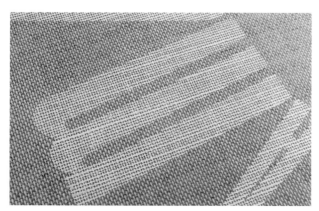

MORUBA
LE NATUREL

Le Naturel, as the name suggests, is a wine created without the introduction of any sulfites or preservatives. Vintae, the Spanish producers of the wine, commissioned Moruba, a graphic design studio based in La Rioja, to create an innovative packaging design that is reminiscent of that used for organic wines while also defining its own bold personality.

As Javier Euba, the founder of Moruba, explains, 'Since we considered this wine as just wine, we wanted to reflect that in the design. The design needed to be simple, but also interesting. We didn't just want to create a simple design for no reason and the simplicity is rooted in the concept: fresh wine with a 'best before' date. We always try to solve our designs with the minimum elements needed. With this design, just using bold black typography was enough to convey this message.'

Focusing on the wine's 'best before' date as the only graphic element on the label is a new concept, especially as wine does not expire, although it does lose some of its qualities. By placing the date in the middle of the label in a larger typesize than the brand identity, it grabs the consumer's attention and clearly communicates the significance of not adding any preservatives.

Publisher Vintae
Art Direction & Design
Daniel Morales, Javier Euba (Moruba)
Production Tea
Origin Spain

DAVID BLAMEY AND JULIA
CONTINUOUS TONE

Continuous Tone is a new sound project by London-based Open Editions, an independent platform for creative partnerships founded by David Blamey. It is intended as a space for enhancing awareness of the aural in relation to the visual. The project invites 12 artists to create a new work pressed onto a 12-inch vinyl record, issued in an edition of 500 copies and a download.

Each issue, with artwork designed by London design studio Julia, contains specially commissioned liner notes inserted as a ten-page illustrated booklet. The first release, *Rural* by David Blamey, features two tracks: 'Wait for It' and 'Nothing Happens'. They are compositions of environmental sounds recorded in the French countryside that reveal something unexpected about situations that, either through over-familiarity or detachment, we are gradually becoming desensitized to.

In Blamey's words, 'The minimalist approach is in keeping with the ethos and look of my work. There is a more conventional photographic image included, but that is placed on the cover of the record sleeve. Because of the contrast between the richness of the full-colour photograph and the simplicity of the typography, the simple act of withdrawing the sleeve from the cover becomes a little "event".'

Publisher Open Editions
Art Direction & Design David Blamey, Julia
Photography David Blamey
Production Identity
Origin UK

THOMAS DANTHONY
N

Satisfying his need to work away from the computer, French illustrator Thomas Danthony embarked on a self-initiated project to create images using only graphite and ink. Initially inspired by the quotation 'The Nape is a mystery to the eye', coined by French author Paul Valéry, the resulting series of 13 drawings was also inspired by the desire to create work about mystery, women, beauty, fashion and simplicity. The drawings were compiled in a black-and-white book, *N*, which was intentionally created with an industrial feel.

There was a standard edition and a luxury edition with a limited-edition, hand-crafted cover with the edition number stamped on it. In Danthony's words, 'As minimalism and simplicity were key elements in the illustrations and design of the book, I wanted to stay on that line (N is for Nape). The black and white colours reflect the medium of the drawings.'

Illustration Thomas Danthony
Origin France

HVASS&HANNIBAL
UNDERVÆRKER

'Underværker – Bygningsarvens Ildsjæle' is a campaign initiated by Realdania, a private philanthropic organization based in Denmark, which promotes the work of enthusiasts with built environments for the benefit of the local community. A book featuring the work of Copenhagen-based graphic design studio Hvass&Hannibal was published to celebrate the projects funded through the campaign.

The technical world of construction is shown in the cover design, which features small symbols that reference building techniques. The simplified black-and-white front cover contrasts with the colourful, geometric back: one symbolizes the technical aspect of a project and the other the personal drive of the people behind it.

Publisher Realdania
Art Direction Hvass&Hannibal
Design Hvass&Hannibal, Sarah Gottlieb
Production Tarm Bogtryk
Origin Denmark

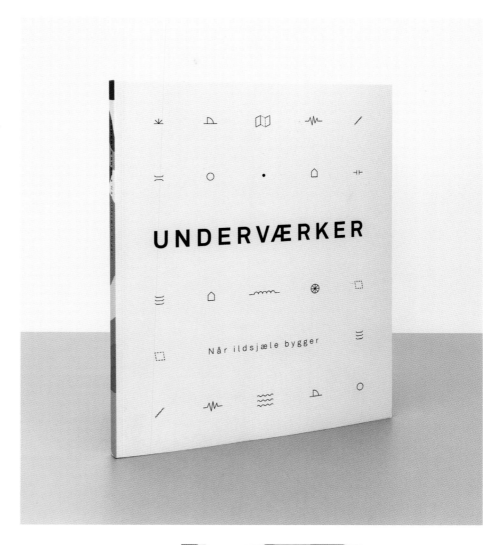

KOREFE
L'EAUNDRY

Love to relax in a hot bath after a long day? Indulging yourself with the finest essences and cleansers and a dash of delicious perfume. You deserve it, and so does your laundry. Because what's the point of buying great clothes if you treat them like old rags? L'eaundry is a premium detergent formulated to gently cleanse and pamper your finest fabrics, rounded off with the subtle fragrance of aromatic figs. To treat your second skin the way skin should be treated

Ingredients: 15–30% anionic surfactants, under 5% non-ioni substances, linalool, benzisothiazolinone, methylisoth...

Recommended amounts:
4,5kg washing machine

Water hardness
soft 0–8,4°d...

L'EAUNDRY is a luxury laundry detergent that smells and looks like a high-class perfume. Released by The Deli Garage, a food cooperative from Hamburg, the product encourages users to treat their clothing as they would their skin – by pampering it.

The association with perfumery is echoed in the bold black-and-white packaging design influenced by vintage chemists' bottles. Created by Hamburg-based Korefe – the Korefe (Kolle Rebbe Form und Entwicklung) is an integrated design agency of Kolle Rebbe – the simplified design establishes the connection to washing agents while the typography and formal style fully evoke the world of fine scents. The detergent is available in two versions: Figue pour femme and Olibanum pour homme.

Publisher The Deli Garage
Creative Director Christian Doering
Design Katharina Ullrich, Christian Doering
Copywriter Lorenz Ritter
Project Manager Shari Linthe
Production KAWE GmbH & Co.
Origin Germany

RUMORS
RADICAL THINKERS

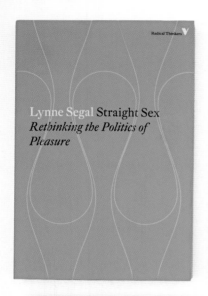

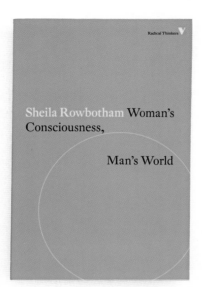

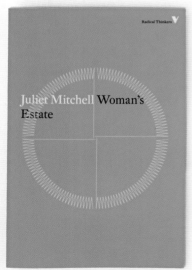

'Radical Thinkers' is a paperback series of works by notable left-wing political and philosophical writers published by Verso Books. Three sets of four books are published annually. This has meant a long-term commitment for the US design studio Rumors, as founder Andy Pressman notes: 'to date we've designed 84 titles.'

Working on a series like this presents the designer with an unusual challenge – to bring coherence and resonance to titles that need to be visually linked and will span several years. Pressman has developed a strict system of type and simple line illustrations, which he brings to bear on each new title. He favours simplicity: 'the covers feature simple illustrations that try to stay true to the spirit of each text. Some of the illustrations are literal and easily "read", while others are abstract representations of slippery ideas.' He avoids the usual design conceits used to demonstrate 'radical' works, such as aggressive colour palettes, 'shouty' typography and 'torn paper'.

Publisher Verso Books
Design Andy Pressman (Rumors)
Production Maple Vail
Origin UK

EDITED
DIEGETIC MUSIC/SOUND,NON-DIEGETIC MUSIC/SOUND

Diegetic Music/Sound and *Non-Diegetic Music/Sound* are a two-volume series by Angela Law dedicated to the study of how music can complement films to create a complete sensory experience. The series has a unified design that seeks to convey cinematography through the use of greyscale gradation, representing light and shadow in film. *Diegetic Music/Sound* portrays our inner selves while *Non-Diegetic Music/Sound* depicts our surroundings and external environments.

The simplicity of Edited's design is enhanced by the hot-stamping effect of the title and the debossed the cover with a tipped-on photograph.

Publisher Kubrick
Art Direction Renatus Wu (Edited)
Design & Illustration Chiu Sung Ying
Production Sun Wah Printing Factory Limited
Origin Hong Kong

ALBERT ROMAGOSA DESIGN CABINET
RETRATS SENSE SOSTRE

Retrats Sense Sostre is a social and cultural art project in Barcelona that aims to give homeless people a voice through art, research and communication.

Curated by Albert Soler and published by The Network of Homeless Care, *Retrats Sense Sostre* includes 12 multi-disciplinary portraits of 12 homeless people made by 12 different artists in 12 different spots around Barcelona. The various graphic responses display the content without hierarchy, which makes everything have the same importance – unlike homeless people, who are often overlooked.

To create an immediately recognizable mark, a responsive arrow/anchor design was conceived to convey a 'stay here' message: the arrow represents 'here' and the anchor 'stay'. As Albert Romagosa from Barcelona-based Albert Romagosa Design Cabinet, who was commissioned to create the design, explains, 'I never thought about a minimalist design while doing it, I was just trying to make it look "normal" and accessible; easy to read and to comprehend. I guess this mentality drove me to the reduced colour palette, using black and white for the most important information (text) and yellow for the anchor/arrow which remains in the background.'

Publisher The Network of Homeless Care
Art Direction & Design Albert Romagosa Design Cabinet
Curator Albert Soler
Origin Spain

78

Retrats Sense Sostre ○ 13–30 Nov. 2014 ○ 12 històries ○ Diversos espais de Bcn ○ Anna Maria ○ Petula Alma ○ William Sabas ○ Miquel Fuster ○ Josep Maria ○ Carlos Blanco ○ Francisco Javier Andrés ○ Elena Fabregat ○ Família Martínez ○ Fernando José Cardenas ○ Miguel Batista ○ Viacheslav Agafonov

#retratsss

retratssensesostre.org

FEED
IN A POST WORLD (A POST-PUNK EVENT)

In a post world, a post-punk event brought together seven Canadian artists, many of whose works are linked to the ideology, ethics and aesthetics of the punk movement, which was notorious for its irreverent spirit and subversion of established cultural and political structures.

For the event, Montreal-based graphic design studio Feed developed a new typeface called 'Youth Grotesque' (released in 2016) that encapsulated their interpretation of the spirit of punk. As Feed co-founder Anouk Pennel explains, 'Following the context of the exhibition, Youth Grotesque was a take on what a post-punk typeface could be. I basically use Monotype Grotesque and other historical references as a main inspiration and add odd contrasting geometric features to it, always keeping in mind the legibility.'

After designing the identity for the exhibition, the studio were asked to contribute a series of posters. Using the typeface as the main material, the installation was a set of five posters that show each weight of the font, in the manner of a specimen sheet. Pennel continues, 'The limitation of the black and white was as much a stylistic statement as a practical device. It fits very well the DIY attitude of the project and also the limited budget. The black and white was also a natural choice for displaying the typeface as it was the core element of the whole design. Punks don't wear pink, you know.'

Curator Pesot Organisme de Création
Art Direction & Design Anouk Pennel, Raphaël Daudelin (Feed)
Production Charmant & Courtois, La Bourgeoise, MP Repro
Origin Canada

MAAN
NOVUM

novum is a monthly German magazine that focuses on graphic design, typography and illustration. When planning the covers, art director Dominic Brighton and editor Christine Moosmann always look for something that has a reference to the topic of the *novum* plus section. For the non-profit issue, the cover, created by Portuguese graphic design studio MAAN, conveys connections, human trust and communication through a minimalist approach based on

a moiré pattern. It is an optical illusion created when repeated graphic patterns are arranged closely to one another.

As Pedro Lima Ferreira, design partner at MAAN, explains, 'By superimposing two half-tone grids 0° to 50° we managed to create an interference visual pattern that gave us the idea of two dependent structures. The metallic pantone metaphorically represents money (copper penny) and contrasts with subtle colours to represent the beginning of 2015.'

The paper, Kristallkarton (by Antalis), is white and metallic ink (copper) was used to print parts of the cover.

Publisher Stiebner Verlag
Art Direction Dominic Brighton
Editor Christine Moosmann
Cover Design Pedro Lima Ferreira, Vitor Claro (MAAN)
Production Kessler Druck + Medien
Origin Germany

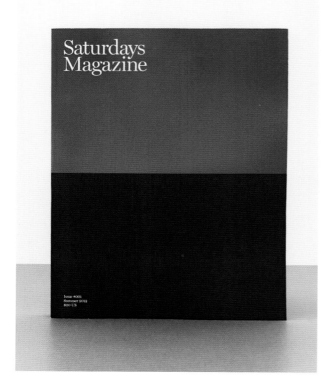

COLIN TUNSTALL
SATURDAYS NYC

Saturdays NYC is a surfing and lifestyle brand based in Manhattan, New York, which cultivates a mix of menswear, art and coffee.

Saturdays NYC produce a surfing and lifestyle publication called *Saturdays Magazine*, which explores the relationship between a city lifestyle and surfing and promotes their stores in New York and Japan – in Tokyo, Kobe, Nagoya and Osaka.

The editorial content reflects the liveliness and adrenalin-associated nature of surf culture through a series of photo essays, interviews and features, while two-tone blocked colours, often in a special fifth colour, are a reflection of Saturdays NYC's brand ethos. As Colin Tunstall, art director for Saturdays NYC, explains, 'The magazine reflects our brand. Our brand centres around balance and this is reflected in the two-tone cover design. Live/work, the city/the beach. It's about finding balance.'

Publisher Saturdays NYC
Owner & Creative Director Colin Tunstall
Design Colin Tunstall, Javas Lehn, Luke Flynn
Production Oddi
Origin USA

Saturdays
Magazine

Issue #004
Spring 2015
$25 US

DAVID LANE
GOURMAND GROTESQUE 777 & 888

The Gourmand, an independent food, arts and culture journal, collaborated with international type house Monotype to design two new bespoke typefaces to be used exclusively in their print and online editions. The new designs, Grotesque 777 and Grotesque 888, reference elements from seven different grotesque typefaces, all designed by Monotype in the 20th century. *The Gourmand*'s creative director David Lane drew on the attributes of each of the different designs to build the new typefaces.

To celebrate the collaboration, *The Gourmand* produced a limited-edition type sample book, matching the dimensions and exacting quality of the journal. Printed on coloured Fedrigoni papers in a rich black ink, with a foil-blocked cover, it also functions as a cookbook, featuring some of the more interesting recipes from previous issues. As David Lane explains, 'It was a logical link as we are a food and culture journal and the typefaces were designed specifically for us. We also wanted to offer an additional layer of editorial information and interest.'

Aside from a pull-out photographic poster, *The Hungry Sinner* by Gustav Almestål, each recipe is presented in an intentionally typography-only format to make sure the focus is only on the typeface design.

Publisher The Gourmand & Monotype
Creative Direction David Lane
Design David Lane, Oliver Long
Typeface Design Gunnar Vilhjalmsson (Monotype)
Editor Marina Tweed
Photography Gustav Almestål
Origin UK

DESIGNERS UNITED
5 OLIVE OIL

5 Olive Oil make a premium line of products from Koroneiki olive crops which are grown in the Peloponnese, Greece. Known for the low acidity in its soil, it is an area with 4,000 years of history in olive-oil production.

Designers United, a brand identity studio in Thessaloniki, were commissioned to create a brand design that reflects the product's premium quality and purity. The branding features simple typography and a minimalist, partly obscured logo that focuses on the number five, which is associated with quintessence in olive oil. The design adorns the simple round bottles, available in a matte black or white, which were developed by Italian glass packaging experts Vetroelite to replicate the shape of old Greek potion bottles, reinforcing the link with traditional olive-oil production.

Publisher World Excellent Products S.A.
Art Direction Designers United
Industrial Design Vetroelite
Brand Strategist Dimitris Panagiotidis
Origin Greece

FIVE
Organic
Extra Virgin Olive Oil
Huile d'olive organique
vierge extra
500ml ℮ 16.9 fl oz

FIVE
Ultra Premium
Extra Virgin Olive Oil
Huile d'olive ultra-premium
vierge extra
500ml ℮ 16.9 fl oz

SECTION.D
PARABOL ART MAGAZINE

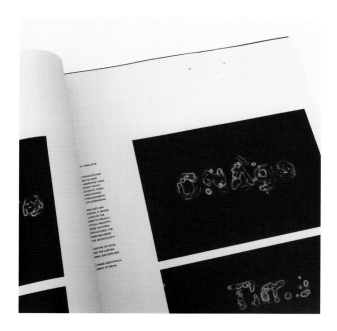

Parabol Art Magazine is a biannual contemporary art magazine which has a different curator assigned to each issue. The curator's task is to examine a contemporary phenomenon using pictures and words on the basis of artistic points of view and to encourage debate about contemporary art.

Created by the Austrian design agency Section.d and the art consultancy Section.a, *Parabol*'s origins and format are unconventional. Measuring 594 mm x 841 mm when folded out, it is almost A1 and seems more like an art catalogue than a traditional magazine.

This individualist spirit, coupled with the logistical problems of an incredibly large format, has resulted in the unique approach of releasing each magazine in its own bag produced in a different material. The 'Retooling' issue, curated by German conceptual artist Peter Weibel, was housed in a bag painted in metallic silver. As Max Haupt-Stummer, creative partner at Section.d, explains, 'Due to the not really small size, it is first necessary to be able to transport the magazine, second it gives each issue a special approach. We use different materials every time with different printing techniques to get the most exciting results.'

Publisher Max Haupt-Stummer, Robert Jasensky (Section.d)
Art Direction Max Haupt-Stummer, Chris Goennawein (Section.d)
Curator Peter Weibel (Karlsruhe)
Design Chris Goennawein
Project Manager Katharina Boesch
Production 08/16 Printproduction
Origin Austria

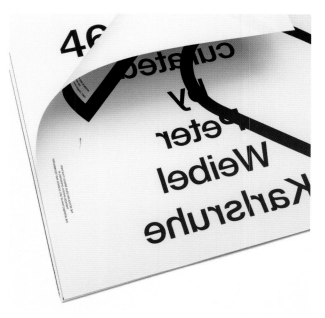

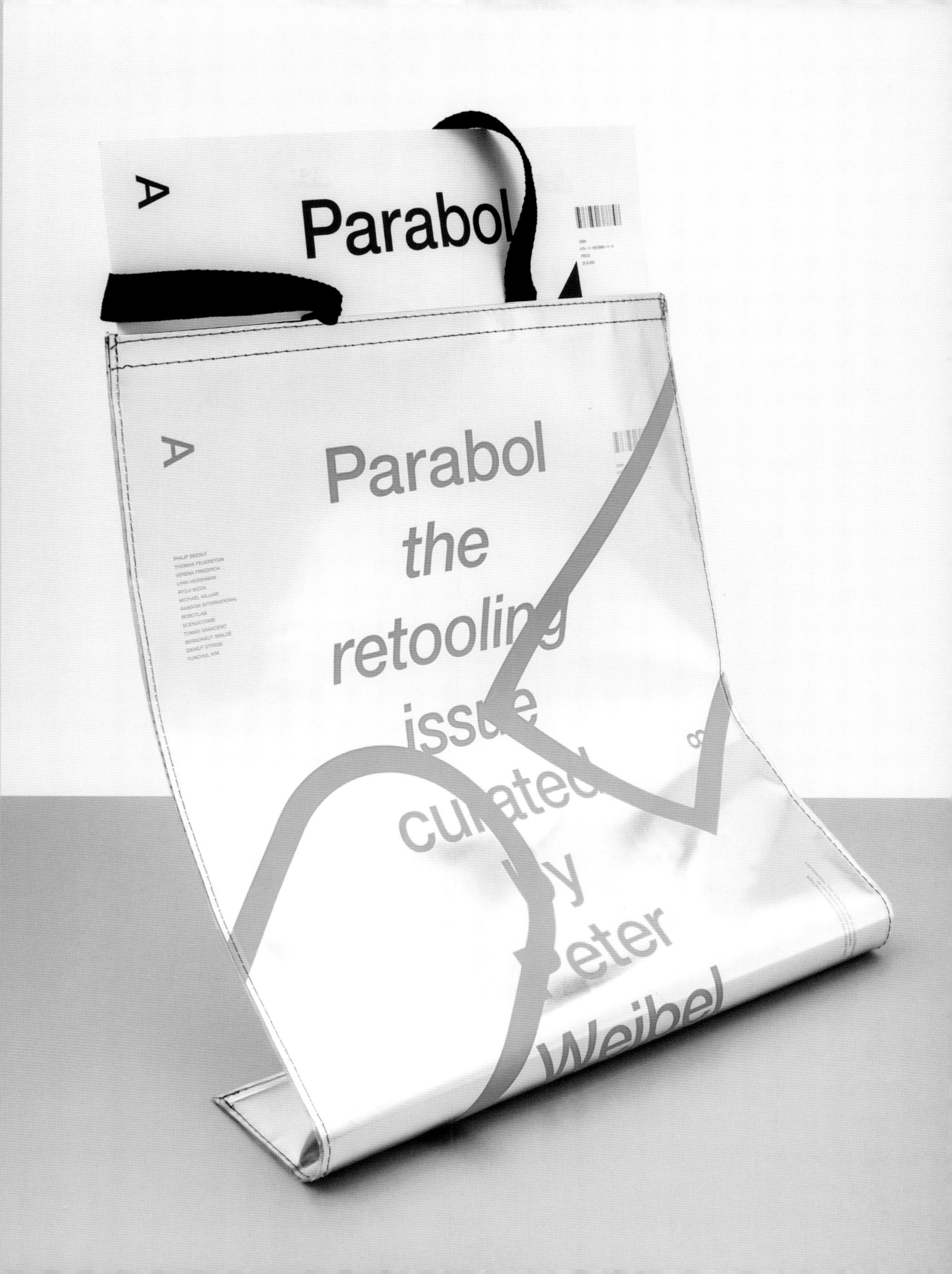

A

Parabol

A

Parabol
the
retooling
issue
curated
by
Peter
Weibel

PHILIP BEESLEY
THOMAS FEUERSTEIN
VERENA FRIEDRICH
LYNN HERSHMAN
AYDU IKEDA
MICHAEL NAJJAR
RANDOM INTERNATIONAL
ROBOTLAB
SCENOCOSME
TOMÁS SARACENO
SERGEAUT SMILDE
GRIMUT STREGE
YUNCHUL KIM

KASPER-FLORIO
STICKEREI

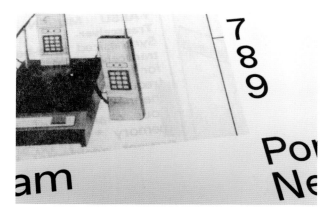

Based in St Gallen in Switzerland, Stickerei is a restaurant-bar and sometimes a live music venue. To advertise upcoming events, Stickerei commission local graphic design studio Kasper-Florio to create posters. The simple poster designs are based on a grid system that highlights the date, time, artist and location of the event. The grid system is deliberately flexible so that information can be easily updated. As Rosario Florio, graphic partner at Kasper-Florio, puts it, 'The idea was to have a flexible system and a unique look that enables easy implementation by just changing the content into the right position. Different information has to be displayed on every poster, so we decided to show all the possible numbers or the initials of the week days.'

Art Direction & Design Larissa Kasper, Rosario Florio (Kasper-Florio)
Origin Switzerland

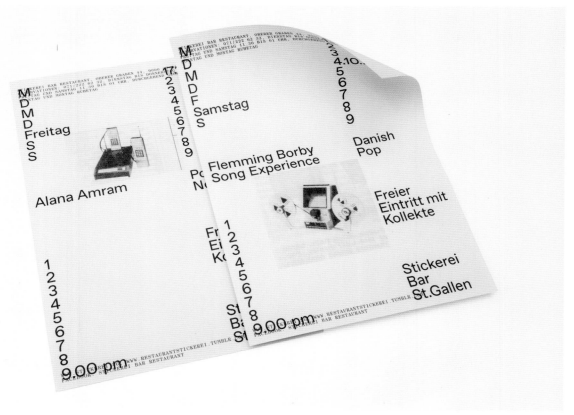

COMMISSION
SEVERAL

Several are a London-based menswear label with a retail space. A design consultancy and e-commerce store as well, they curate understated clothing lines that focus on modernity, craftsmanship and quiet luxury influenced by UK sub-cultures. When commissioning the brand design, Several approached London-based branding consultancy Commission.

The graphic vocabulary of the brand is quiet with a strong focus on material and technique. The black-and-white palette creates a consistent foundation for the identity, and individuality is expressed on gift vouchers and swing tickets, where the edges are hand-dipped in ink.

The symbol of the semi-colon is used to convey the idea of 'several': distinct items that are part of the collective. It also forms the basis of the logo – the Several sun – a mark designed to be subtly reproduced in unexpected places.

When a small pop of colour is applied it becomes all the more powerful, given the neutral nature of the rest of the identity. This is evident in the aw.15 collection, which references a nautical fishing theme. The tote bag utilizes a bright 'safety orange' colour found on buoys at sea.

Art Direction & Design Commission
Origin UK

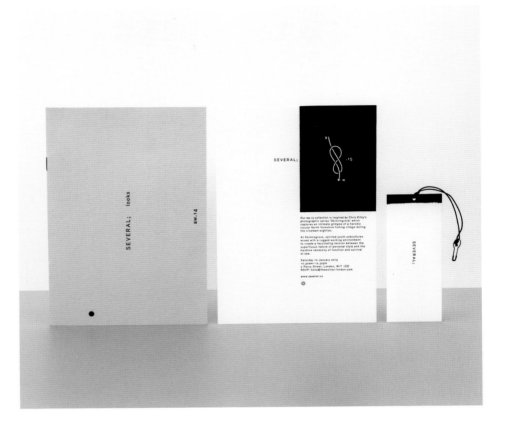

GENÍS CARRERAS
NEW PHILOSOPHER

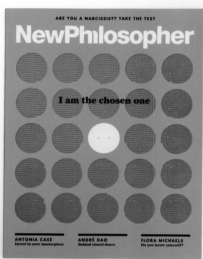

New Philosopher is an independent quarterly magazine published in Australia, devoted to exploring philosophical ideas from past and present thinkers on ways to live a more fulfilling life. Each issue is curated according to a theme (such as mind, self, health, growth or happiness) which is cleverly reflected in the simple cover design created by London-based illustrator Genís Carreras.

The cover direction aims to bring philosophy to a global audience. The use of simple, minimalist graphics speaks to readers from different cultural and linguistic backgrounds.

The series of simple graphics, realized in brilliant colours, sparks ideas and engages the reader in thinking about the topic more deeply.

Publisher The Bull Publishing
Art Direction Carlos Egan, Aida Novoa
Cover Illustration Genís Carreras
Production Offset Alpine, Quad/Graphics
Origin Australia

WHY THE PURSUIT OF HAPPINESS IS MAKING US SAD

NewPhilosopher

Are we happy yet?

CLIVE HAMILTON
Happiness and all that crap

OLIVER BURKEMAN
The perils of positive thinking

DAMON YOUNG
Happiness is hard to find

SOCIAL REVOLUTION

The years from 1914 to 1918, when the First World War was fought, were one of the most horrific periods in the history of mankind – but, despite this destruction, also one of the most innovative, spawning multiple new art forms and producing one of the most radical artworks ever painted.
By Stuart Tolley

A minimalist approach to art, based on restraint and order, is recognized as a 20th-century movement that can be traced back over a century to the anarchic years during the First World War. This was a period of revolution and modernization through machines, and there was a desire to re-create society from the ashes of the 'Great War'. But the origins of simplification have slightly more humble beginnings, which can be found in late 18th-century England, where the 'Shaker' religion was founded, and later in America, once the Shakers had emigrated.

Shakers, named after a spiritual dance that saw believers shake during worship, followed a religion that was an amalgamation of existing religions followed by Methodists, Quakers and Camisards. Shakers practised living a perfect Christian life through celibacy, utility and simplicity, in preparation for Christ's second coming. Although founded in England, it wasn't until the Shakers emigrated to America in 1774 that the religion was widely practised. They quickly established large-scale communes and within a century there were 6,000 members spread over 18 such groups.

These communes were largely self-sufficient, affording the Shakers little contact with the outside world and its corrupting influences. In their homes Shakers followed the same simple principles where every object should have function and be devoid of unnecessary ornamentation or decoration, which was believed to encourage sin. Emphasis was placed on functionality, quality and craftsmanship, with the mantra that 'beauty rests on utility'. Shakers didn't take individual credit for their creations, which is why no names are attached to the style, but their furniture is instead recognizable by its simple minimalist beauty, practicality and extremely high quality. This belief was summed up as follows: 'Don't make something unless it is both necessary and useful; but if it is both necessary and useful, don't hesitate to make it beautiful.'

It was not, however, until the early 20th century, during the horrors of the First World War and the dawn of the machine age, that simplification, geometry and abstraction began to inform the visual arts. At the turn of the 20th century machines were a source of optimism: an exciting tomorrow promised a cleaner, more efficient, mass-produced world. People had already taken to the skies and progressive inventions such as the automobile were becoming part of the modern way of life, introducing the concept of mass production. Almost a century later, this sense of progress and modernization is not hard to imagine in our own lives as we walk unguided into the digital age. Authors Erik Brynjolfsson and Andrew McAfee argue that we have already entered a second machine age, where machines have developed so far that they now perform tasks originally only carried out by humans, such as in medicine, science and the service industry.

During the build-up to the First World War there was a great desire for social change, and a need to eradicate the old guard and the social structures they governed. This radical new strain of thought was based on the idea that society needed to be completely revolutionized. For the first time, man was questioning his own mortality and the role of religion in society. Charles Darwin published *On the Origin of Species* to much furore in 1859, and in his second book, *The Descent of Man, and Selection in Relation to Sex*, outlined his theories on human evolution, which were contrary to religious belief and used the term 'evolution' for the first time. These radical viewpoints were accentuated in the writing of the German philosopher Friedrich Nietzsche, who famously proclaimed 'God is dead' and questioned the role of Christianity in society.

During this period artists abandoned traditional subjects such as religion, landscape and portraiture in favour of abstraction, disruption and an alternate perspective. Cubist painters such as Pablo Picasso and Georges Bracque revolutionized art by re-examining subjects through multiple viewpoints that were rearranged and later amalgamated as sculptures or painted onto canvas. These paintings rejected traditional rules about perspective that had been standard for over 500 years. Machines, mechanical movement and mass production proved an inspiration for a number of avant-garde artists, such as the Italian Futurists, who aimed to encapsulate this raw energy, technology and speed in their artwork. In the words of Filippo Marinetti, 'We want to fight ferociously against the fanatical, unconscious and snobbish religion of the past, which is nourished by the evil influence of museums. We rebel against the supine admiration of old canvases, old statues and old objects, and against the enthusiasm for all that is worm-eaten,

dirty and corroded by time; we believe that the common contempt for everything young, new and palpitating with life is unjust and criminal.'

But all of this was set to change with the assassination of Archduke Franz Ferdinand of Austria in 1914 and the outbreak of the First World War. The subsequent period of true horror shattered the prevailing optimism of a modernized society with machines at its heart, and instilled the need to revolutionize its very foundations. This was an era of great social divides between the governing upper classes and the lower working classes, and this was nowhere more evident than in the trenches, where examples of the troops being treated like little more than cattle are widely documented. The popular phrase 'lions led by donkeys' summed up the contrast between the courage of the infantry and the haplessness of their leaders. The unprecedented death toll among the infantry can easily be blamed on the reckless leadership of the upper classes, but this was a new type of war, the first to use machines in battle, and was uncharted waters for generals and infantry alike.

The role of the machine was pivotal to the outcome of the war. In 1914 the aeroplane was a very basic machine with no navigation equipment. Planes were mostly used for reconnaissance missions and more pilots were killed in training than in combat. But after the outbreak of the war they were rapidly transformed into sophisticated fighting machines used for plane-on-plane combat, and were also developed into rudimentary bombers.

'The First World War traumatized a generation, but the anger towards the authoritarian upper classes became a source of inspiration for a new generation of artists. Dada, a literary and artistic movement formed in 1916 in neutral Switzerland, was created by a group of anarchic artists.'

Despite the mechanization of war, many of the killing machines at the disposal of generals were in their infancy. Quick-fire weapons such as machine guns were cumbersome objects that required a team of six to make them work. They could fire about 500 rounds of small ammunition per minute, but by 1918 this amount had doubled. When first presented to the British army by its inventor, the American Hiram Maxim, the new machine gun was dismissed, as it was seen to be of little use. Germany, on the other hand, seized the opportunity and by the outbreak of the war had 12,000 machine guns at its disposal. These new fighting machines were used against 'men in trenches' defences, but communication was poor and radio was in its infancy.

New methods of warfare were being developed around the front line. Aeroplanes and tanks were pivotal to the success of the Battle of Amiens, the first tier of offensives by British forces which ultimately led to victory over Germany. This battle optimized the role of the machine in warfare: British, French, Canadian and Australian troops, led by tank divisions and protected by aerial bombardment from aeroplanes, advanced eight miles during the course of the battle – a very significant distance at the time. This battle demonstrated how an army

led by machines could be effective, and signalled the extent of the army's revolution; it has since become the blueprint for contemporary warfare.

Despite the gradual modernization of society and the early days of mass communication, the First World War was clouded with censorship. This meant the true horrors were never realized by those at home. For many, the only way to express this horror was through amateur writing, poetry and art. Many of the artists practising at the time were employed by the state to portray the war, but under strict censorship. One of these artists was the painter Paul Nash, who commented in 1917, 'I have just returned last night from a visit to Brigade Headquarters up the line and I shall not forget it as long as I live. I am no longer an artist interested and curious, I am a messenger who will bring back word from the men who are fighting to those who want the war to go on for ever. Feeble, inarticulate, will be my message, but it will have a bitter truth, and may it burn their lousy souls.'

The First World War traumatized a generation, but the anger towards the authoritarian upper classes became a source of inspiration for a new generation of artists. Dada, a literary and artistic movement formed in 1916 in neutral

'This revolutionary spirit was perfectly encapsulated by the Russian artist Kazimir Malevich and his painting *Black Square*, which was created in 1915.'

Switzerland, was created by a group of anarchic artists who regularly met at a club called the Cabaret Voltaire in Zurich to discuss and perform spoken-word pieces voicing their hatred of the war. Dadaist work was not unified by a style, but was driven by an angry reaction to everything the war stood for. Their aim was to overthrow the old guard and create new forms of visual art that reflected their vision of a new world free from the killing machines. One leading Dadaist, Jean Arp, summed up this hatred: 'Repelled by the slaughterhouses of war, we turned to art. We searched for an elementary art that would, we thought, save mankind from the furious madness of the times.'

In Russia, inspired by a revulsion towards the First World War and the desire to overthrow the Tsarist classes, who ruled Russia at the time, artists created a new style of painting that rejected the formalities of fine art, such as the easel, in favour of abstract works that announced the death of traditionalism. These works were created to voice the misery of the daily life of the masses and the belief that art can transcend this common struggle and inspire change.

This revolutionary spirit was perfectly encapsulated by the Russian artist Kazimir Malevich and his painting *Black Square*, which was created in 1915. Malevich was born in 1879 into a working-class family of Ukrainian and Polish origin and spent much of his childhood travelling around while his parents searched for work. Pursuing a late interest in art, which saw him adopting painting methods used in local peasant folk art, Malevich enrolled at the Kiev School of Art in 1895 and later studied at the Moscow School of Painting.

By 1913, Malevich had aligned himself with such like-minded artists and poets as the Russian Futurists Velimir Khlebnikov and Aleksei Kruchenykh, who were interested in pursuing a more philosophical approach to art. Between 1907 and 1912 they collaborated on a series of books and plays, with set design by Malevich, which reflected the complexities of the Western European–Russian relationship during the period of uncertainty in preparation for the war. Famously, one of these theatre backdrops was thought to be an early version of Malevich's *Black Square*, and led the artist to retrace the origins of the painting, which he later dated to 1913, at the time of the play, instead of 1915, when it was first exhibited. It was around this time that Malevich started to conceive of the concept of reducing painting to its purest form – free from the representational shackles of traditional art. He wanted the painting to be viewed as an object in its own right. This concept took another two years to formulate, but the result was seen in one of the most shockingly radical paintings ever created in the 20th century.

Black Square was first exhibited at the 'Last Futurist Exhibition of Paintings 0.10' in St Petersburg. The exhibition featured other abstract works, such as *Black Cross*, but the artwork that was most celebrated was an imperfect black square painted inside a completely white painted canvas. As Malevich said, 'The black square on the white field was the first form in which nonobjective feeling came to be expressed. The square = feeling, the white field = the void beyond this feeling.'

This painting symbolizes the death of art as a representational medium through the portrayal of complete blankness. Malevich's new art style was called Suprematism, proclaiming that this new art was far superior to all art of the past and would lead to the 'supremacy of pure feeling or perception in the pictorial art.'

Breaking with exhibition convention, *Black Square* was not arranged in a white-walled gallery environment, but instead was pinned to the wall, unframed and misaligned. Other abstract geometric artworks adorned the walls of the exhibition, but *Black Square* was hung highest of all and spanned the corner of two walls, traditionally an area reserved in the Russian home for the hanging of Orthodox Christian religious icons. At the time this approach was shocking. The aim of the exhibition, which was hinted at through the exhibition title,

was to signal the end of painting, but instead it ushered in the beginning of a new approach to fine art, which was centred around geometric form and abstraction.

Malevich's work was extremely inspirational and he explored the concept of Suprematist, non-representational art for a further five years. By this time, in 1917, the Russian Revolution had began in St Petersburg with the aim of overthrowing the traditional Tsarist autocracy, a regime that was opposed to the modernized world and had strict governance over its people, who had little freedom of expression. Revolutionaries wanted to replace the old guard with a Bolshevik government, later to become the Communist party, which would represent the working and peasant classes.

Malevich's use of non-representational imagery and geometric form greatly influenced the Russian artist, designer, typographer, architect and photographer El Lissitzky, who was born in 1890 in the south-eastern corner of Russia to a middle-class Jewish family. He tried to enrol in the St Petersburg School of Art, but despite having the necessary qualifications he was unable to join because the ruling Tsarist regime only allowed a small number of Jewish pupils to attend Russian universities. This pivotal moment in the young man's life forced him to leave Russia for the first time and to enrol at the Technical Academy of Art in Germany to study architectural engineering.

Fuelled by the grievances he felt against the anti-semitic beliefs of the Tsarist regime, El Lissitzky became involved with the Jewish nationalist movement, which sought to revive Yiddish culture among Russian Jews. It was during this time that he started to illustrate children's books that communicated traditional Jewish culture to a younger generation. He was developing a graphic language that he called 'goal-oriented creation', in the belief that design and architecture can inspire social change.

In 1919 El Lissitzky started creating propaganda posters that voiced his hostility towards war and his support for the Bolshevik government in the hope of a new modern Russian order. He was living in Vitebsk in Belarus, where he was joined by Malevich. At the time the pair were experimenting with Suprematism, despite the venomous reception they received from local artists, who preferred traditional figurative painting. El Lissitzky started to incorporate architectural forms into his geometric 'Proun' paintings, developing a graphic visual language that eventually became Constructivism. It was during their time in Vitebsk that the pair started to take over the art-school system and distributed crudely produced propaganda posters in support of the Bolshevik revolution, which incorporated geometric shapes to communicate their message to the largely illiterate peasant population, who were not afforded education under the Tsarist regime.

Modernization and revolution were the driving forces behind El Lissitzky's graphic style. He stated at the time, 'The sun as the expression of old world energy is torn down from the heavens by modern man, who by virtue of his technological superiority creates his own energy source.' His most recognizable poster, an early attempt at revolutionary symbolism, is *Beat the Whites with the Red Wedge*, created in 1919. The propaganda 'call to action' poster features black, white and red geometric shapes which graphically represent the revolutionary stance of the Red Wedge (Bolshevik) penetration of the White Army, who were opposed to the revolution.

Beat the Whites with the Red Wedge was littered with graphic symbolism. The red, black and white colours alone represent revolution, while the red (Communist) arrow defiantly penetrates the white (Tsarist) circle. In today's visually educated environment, the symbolism of the 'red wedge penetrating the white circle' is clear, but it is very unlikely that this message was recognized by the peasant population at the time, as the graphic language was so new and revolutionary. It did, however, contribute to the overthrowing of the Tsarist regime, which signalled the beginning of the Russian Communist era under Lenin.

El Lissitzky's Constructivist graphic language has had a profound effect on graphic designers since 1919, and we are fortunate to live in the world to which the Suprematists, Futurists and Constructivists aspired. El Lissitzky's artwork is now a symbol in its own right and is an immediate visual reference for revolution, but more recently it has adorned the commercial formats of record and book covers.

In the 1970s and early 1980s this graphic language was revived in the British punk and new wave movements, a music,

'El Lissitzky's Constructivist graphic language has had a profound effect on graphic designers since 1919, and we are fortunate to live in the world to which the Suprematists, Futurists and Constructivists aspired.'

fashion and art scene with anarchic undertones. Graphic designers such as Barney Bubbles, Malcolm Garrett and Peter Saville immediately recognized the relevance of punk and new wave and created artwork inspired by Constructivism to encapsulate its energetic spirit.

Bubbles, a pioneer of this new graphic style, had previously created psychedelic artwork for bands such as Hawkwind, but after he returned to London at the end of the 1970s he began working as a cover artist with Stiff Records, a record label that had a typically 'anything goes' attitude. Bubbles began to draw on his interest in and readings of post-Russian Revolution Constructivist art to create work that was flat, bright and graphic.

Punk was to have a profound effect on polite British society, which was still in a period of austerity after the loss of Empire in the postwar decades. Although short-lived, punk courted rebellion and freedom of expression through a DIY aesthetic that encompassed music, design and fashion. Today's society is far less inclined towards revolution, but I think it is fitting that the penetrative symbolism and geometric design of *Beat the Whites with the Red Wedge* was referenced in the recent protests against corporate banking in the wake of the financial crash in 2008.

In a stance that echoes the distrust of the Tsarist autocracy, which led to the Russian Revolution a century ago, Occupy London, a grassroots organization, was set up to fight the injustices of the elite corporate banking system. The organization, part of a global network, includes ordinary working people who have felt the injustices first-hand. Since 2011 Occupy London have organized protests with the aim of changing the political and governmental system. After being forced to change their original logo, which looked too similar to the London Underground roundel, they set an open brief for submissions.

The winning design was created by British graphic designer and typographer Jonathan Barnbrook, who is recognized for his social beliefs and work, having created politically motivated posters and art-directed issues of the *Adbusters* magazine. His winning design references the penetrative symbolism of the original poster to include an O being punctured by an arrow which has the tip of an L. El Lissitzky's art was created to inspire revolution and voice hatred towards the elite that governed Russia at the time. It seems fitting, almost a century later, that Barnbrook's design is adorned by an organization representing anger towards the capitalist banking system.

THE GRID

Often misinterpreted as a tool that stifles creativity, the grid has been central to the development of reduced and geometric graphic design for over a century. Originally conceived to aid revolutionary art styles, grids have been used by some of the most inspirational graphic designers.

By Stuart Tolley

'The grid system is an aid, not a guarantee. It permits a number of possible uses and each designer can look for a solution appropriate to his personal style. But one must learn how to use the grid; it is an art that requires practice.' These are the words of Joseph Müller-Brockmann, a Swiss graphic designer.

Grids: love them or hate them, they are a ubiquitous feature in the development of simplified graphic design. If you are reading this book then you are probably interested in grid systems. As an art director, I utilize them in my design work – this book sticks to a set of rules and guides – but I also know when to ignore the grid. This is important, as grids are a tool to enable creativity and composition rather than stifle them. I aim to show over the next few pages how grids have been a tool for creating exciting, inspiring and sometimes revolutionary work.

Grids have been used in the visual arts since the 15th century to help map out canvases and give the illusion of depth and perspective. Before this time, painting was flat. The illusion of perspective was revolutionary at the time, even shocking, but this tool enabled artists to create depth. The basic rules of perspective were used for over 500 years until the early 20th century, when modern artists such as Pablo Picasso and Georges Braque rejected traditional rules and created Cubist paintings that viewed subjects from multiple angles before piecing them together to create new works that appeared to shatter the object.

Inspired by the Cubists' revolutionary new practice, avant-garde artists during the decades around the First World War made flat geometric shapes and a reduced aesthetic central to the development of painting. It was a period when artists, perhaps naively, thought their art could change the governance of the world and many aligned themselves with the political persuasions of their homeland.

This was most evident in Italy. The Futurist artist Filippo Marinetti, who was a leading member of the Fascist movement, created work that represented a new order which dragged Italy away from its stereotypically regressive society. Marinetti's Fascist party later merged with Mussolini's to form the Italian Fascist Party, although Mussolini was never interested in art. Marinetti eventually became disillusioned with Fascism, but his view of war was unwavering: his comment about the Italo–Ethiopian war of 1935 says it all: 'War is beautiful because it initiates the dreamt-of metallization of the human body.'

The art world was predominantly opposed to the war, and the early 20th century was unparalleled in the creation of artistic styles and in voicing opposition to traditional society. This was not only true of artists living and working in war-torn Europe, but also in neutral countries at the time, which included Switzerland and the Netherlands. Despite their neutrality, these countries produced some of the most anarchic, nihilistic artists of the period. Dada, a nihilistic art movement from Switzerland, was strictly focused on reshaping modern society as a reaction to the needless waste of life seen in the First World War. They aimed to burn society and reform it from the ground up. Similarly, in the Netherlands, also a neutral country at this time, artists were inspired by Malevich's non-representational art (see pages 92–99) and formed De Stijl, an abstract art movement and supporting newspaper of the same name, which voiced the artists' theories on art and anti-war literature, and promoted their new art style – called Neo-Plasticism – which was created by the godfather of the geometric grid, Piet Mondrian.

Mondrian was born in Amersfoort, Utrecht, in the north-eastern corner of the Netherlands, and studied painting at the Amsterdam Academy, where he was influenced by other Dutch masters such as Van Gogh as well as by the Pointillist style of the late 19th century. In 1912 he moved to Paris, the centre of the art world at the time, and began experimenting in avant-garde painting after visiting an exhibition by Picasso and Braque. When he returned home at the outbreak of the First World War, Mondrian found himself restricted by the censorship in the Netherlands.

The Netherlands was a neutral country and a world away from Paris, which was in the grip of war. This neutrality afforded artists the opportunity to work uninterrupted, but it was a time clouded in censorship. The press, whose war reportage was heavily censored, were ordered to provide an unbiased perspective, due to the fear of an invasion

and the risk of the country losing its neutral status. Not everyone, however, adhered to this. The anti-German cartoonist Louis Raemaekers, then working for the *De Telegraaf* newspaper, drew an image of the German emperor suggesting he was in allegiance with Satan, describing the German army as 'a band of heartless scoundrels who caused the war'.

It was during this period that a style of art was sweeping through Europe, inspired by Malevich's Suprematism, which began to explore the concept of painting as being non-representational and rejecting traditional subjects. Despite being cut off from other European artists, Mondrian and his fellow Dutch artist Theo van Doesburg set out to create a new abstract approach called Concrete Art, which was created without any figurative or symbolic references. This new style of painting, centred around geometric shapes arranged on a vertical or horizontal axis, was promoted through *De Stijl*.

De Stijl was a thoroughly modern publication, and its universal graphic language was fittingly pared-back, abstract and geometric. Largely typographic, featuring bold sans-serif typography, the new Concrete Art style was emphasized from issue 1 (published in 1917), which featured an abstract geometric block design on the cover. The first issue also featured a new logo, created in 1917 by *De Stijl* founding member Vilmos Huszár, who created the paper's name entirely from geometric square blocks arranged at

'Curves were banished, as a curved line was considered too expressive, and colours were predominantly black and white, but with the use of primary colours: blue, yellow and red.'

90-degree horizontal and vertical angles to form stencil-style lettering. Although only ever printed in runs of 300, *De Stijl* had a profound effect on Dutch art and design, largely because of its grid-based design, straight lines and the geometry of Neo-Plasticism. Curves were banished, as a curved line was considered too expressive, and colours were predominantly black and white, but with the use of primary colours: blue, yellow and red.

After the war, Mondrian began to explore his own grid-based geometric style, with which he is now famously associated, called De Nieuwe Beelding, or 'Neo-Plasticism', which literally means 'new art'. This name was very appropriate after the war as it was a period of significant change in social structure. This new painting only used horizontal and vertical lines on a grid, geometric shape, and primary colours, alongside black and white.

In the first issue of *De Stijl*, Mondrian set out his aspirations for Neo-Plasticism by stating, 'As a pure representation of the human mind, art will express itself in an aesthetically purified, that is to say abstract form. The new plastic idea cannot, therefore, take the form of a natural or concrete representation – this new plastic idea will ignore the particulars of appearance, that is to say, natural form and colour. On the contrary, it should find its expression in the abstraction of form and colour, that is to say, in the straight line and the clearly defined primary colour.' *Composition No. II*, dated 1920, is one of Mondrian's earliest geometric works and shows the artist's development of the use of vertical and horizontal lines and primary colours to reflect his interest in universal order and the philosophical theories of theosophy. This new direction introduced a checker-board grid system, which was applied before oil painting commenced, and which separated the canvas into intersecting horizontal and vertical lines to create compositions. Mondrian's work of the 1920s remains some of the most influential in the development of modern art, but it is a common misconception that Mondrian was only interested in aesthetic beauty. It is easy to forget the shocking impact these paintings had on art – we are now familiar with the grid compositions that have adorned numerous mainstream items, from clothing (Yves Saint Laurent in the 1960s), interior decoration and even cakes. But these paintings were revolutionary, and Mondrian was one of the last significant artists who felt his work would filter through society and art to inspire a new social order.

'Where previous theories of modernization were regional, the new movement was global, and affected all facets of the visual arts. During this period, graphic design was a comparatively new profession.'

His approach was to reduce sections of his previous paintings radically into non-representational abstract compositions that reflected the essence of nature and the universe. His ideas were largely inspired by the mysticism of theosophy and reflected the positive–negative and masculine –feminine dualities of nature. 'Mondrian saw art not as an end, but a means to an end – spiritual clarification', wrote Robert Hughes in *The Shock of the New*. Mondrian was to explore his geometric, grid-based Neo-Plasticist style until his death in 1944, by which time he had fallen out with Van Doesburg. As the legend goes, Van Doesburg started to introduce diagonal lines into his work and so Mondrian disassociated himself from the artist.

Mondrian's work was highly influential in the development of modern art. His and Van Doesburg's ideas for a utopian modern society were never realized, partly because they were overly ambitious, but the development of modern art was thwarted by another setback with the outbreak of the Second World War. This was a period of mass genocide, and the stifling of creativity throughout the world.

The German Nazi party, under the dictatorship of Hitler, aimed to purify German culture and promote classical representations of art – everything the modern avant-garde artists had been rebelling against since Malevich painted *Black Square* in 1915. Hitler sought to close the Bauhaus, a revolutionary German art school that believed in fusing all disciplines of the visual arts, because he believed it was a centre for teaching Communist theories. Hitler began to alienate the Bauhaus in 1933 and immediately put into effect the closure of its original location in Dessau. Within a few years the school was relocated to Berlin, but the path was set and it was closed within a few years. Undeterred, the majority of teachers at the school, including the artist Josef Albers, fled Germany in favour of teaching abroad.

This period was to have a stifling effect on Europe, and indeed the arts, leaving many countries bankrupt and leading to the dissolution of the British Empire, which started with Indian independence in 1947. Once again, Europe had to rebuild itself, and during a period of austerity and food rationing, from the rubble of the bombed-out cities, came a renewed desire to rebuild the social landscape. Central to this philosophy was the grid.

The French architect Le Corbusier had already proposed his ideas for 'towers in the park' in the 1930s. His ideas for a modern grid-based cityscape, which aimed to revolutionize over-crowded and polluted inner cities, gained new ground in the wake of the Second World War. His ideas were to influence town planners and architects for decades, helping to reshape towns in the manner we recognize today.

Where previous theories of modernization were regional, the new movement was global, and affected all facets of the visual arts. During this period, graphic design was a comparatively new profession, without a unified language and predominantly reliant on illustration. Subtlety wasn't a consideration, but this was set to change during the late 1940s and 1950s with the development of the Swiss Design or International Typographic Style by graphic designers Armin Hofmann, Emil Ruder and most notably Josef Müller-Brockmann. These graphic artists, alongside other contemporaries, sought to revolutionize the landscape of design through the use of geometry, photo-montage, grid systems and the removal or reduction of 'unnecessary' illustrative decoration.

What is most notable is that this new language came from a country that was neutral in both of the wars. The unified graphic style that arose in Switzerland was to have a profound effect on the graphic-design community. At times it bordered on modern art, and it was clearly visually influenced by Constructivism and De Stijl. Speaking to *Eye* magazine just before his death in 1996, Müller-Brockmann commented, 'It is a genuine compulsion. The study of art has been one of

my basic needs and I have consciously sought an artist as my companion in life: my first wife, who died tragically early in a car crash, was a musician and my second wife, Shizuko Yoshikawa, is a painter. Concrete Art is the kind of art that appeals to me most directly as a graphic artist. Its principles, which are open to analysis, can be transmuted into graphic terms. Of all the art movements of the 20th century, it is the one that is universal and still open to development. You might say it is the art in which I can discover the fewest flaws.'

One of the most recognized and influential practitioners of the new Swiss Style, Müller-Brockmann was born in 1914 in Switzerland. After graduating from the University of Zurich with qualifications in architecture, design and art history, he opened his first studio in 1936, specializing in graphic design, exhibition graphics and photography. After the outbreak of the Second World War, Müller-Brockmann served in the Swiss army. It was not until the 1950s that he started to create the work for which he is now most eagerly remembered. His most recognized work was created for the Zurich Tonhalle, a concert hall that was built in the late 19th century and is now home to the Tonhalle Orchestra. The hall was celebrated for its superb acoustics, and Müller-Brockmann reflected these harmonies through a series of beautifully constructed minimalist posters that drew on Constructivism and De Stijl. Müller-Brockmann's posters during this period were stripped of superfluous colour and illustration and featured only geometric patterns accompanied by the preferred sans-serif typeface, Akzidenz-Grotesk. The posters were startlingly beautiful, with a perfectly balanced composition that utilized Müller-Brockmann's grid system. The most celebrated poster of this period is the 'Beethoven' design (1955), with broken disks arranged on a circle. In my opinion, the design that epitomizes Müller-Brockmann's love of Concrete Art and composition is *Aus der Sammlung des Kunsthauses Zürich* (1953), with its five rectangular shapes positioned rhythmically over the poster. Similarly to De Stijl, the new Swiss Style had its own publication, *Neue Grafik* (1958–65), which introduced the discipline of graphic design to the world and created a platform for Müller-Brockmann to showcase his (and other contemporaries such as Hans Neuburg and Carlo Vivarelli's) typographic and grid-based designs. The magazine, which was originally published in 18 editions, helped establish the Swiss Style throughout the world, having a monumental effect on graphic design, arguably mostly within the publishing industry.

One of the most successful and inspirational iterations of a unified grid structure was the 'Marber/Penguin Grid' created for Penguin in 1960. Before the Marber Grid, Penguin book covers were haphazard, at best 'drifting from one design to another, diluting Penguin Books' identity, reputation and goodwill.' This was recognized by the Italian graphic designer Germano Facetti, who was the art director at Penguin Books UK from 1961 until 1972. During this period he revolutionized the Penguin book-cover format and helped establish the book publisher as an integral part of British culture.

Born in Milan in 1926, Facetti spent his teenage years under the Fascist regime during the Second World War. In 1943, at the age of 17, he was arrested by the Germans, who suspected he was a member of the Italian Resistance, and he was duly deported to Mauthausen concentration camp, where he spent the rest of the war until its liberation by the Americans in 1944. After the war, Facetti worked in Milan-based architectural practices before leaving for England in 1950, having married a British architect and enrolled on a typography class at Central Saint Martins. He later became an art editor at Aldus Books. His experiences captured his imagination, and he claimed the book-designing process was 'the flow of images, captions and diagrams... planned like a documentary film'. After a period working in France he returned to London as art director at Penguin Books. One of the designer's chief roles was to bring Penguin book covers up to date and help bring a unified framework to each category. This unification process began with the redesign of the Penguin Crime series, where Facetti enlisted the help of British graphic designer Romek Marber in 1961. Marber had previously created grid-based cover designs for *The Economist*. 'The Economist covers I view with nostalgia. They led the way to designing covers for Penguin and ultimately to the redesign of their Crime series covers. Peter Dunbar had been appointed art director of *The Economist*. Up to

'The graphic language of grids is steeped in revolutionary history, but how does it resonate with today's graphic environment? The grid has taken on a new life in the creation of websites and apps, especially as a method for unification.'

then *The Economist* covers had running text and no picture. The printing was in letterpress on newsprint in two colours, red and black', said Marber. His first commission was to unify the Penguin Crime series, and he set about constructing a revolutionary grid system that afforded the cover designer space to create an engaging illustration while keeping the title and author legible in a consistent location at the top of the book. The result was an immediately recognizable cover direction that caught the eye of the discerning reader, re-establishing Penguin as a national treasure. But Marber felt that the success of the initial 20 Crime covers was largely due to the accompanying illustration: 'Much has been made of the grid; it has even been labelled "the Marber grid". I believe that the pictures for the initial 20 covers played an important part in forging the identity of the Crime series. The grid was important as the rational element of control. The consistency of the pictures contributed, as much as the grid, to the unity of the covers, and the dark shadowy photography gave the covers a feel of crime.' The resulting design proved so successful that it was utilized throughout the whole Penguin/Pelican book series and has since become an icon of grid-based design.

The graphic language of grids is steeped in revolutionary history, but how does it resonate with today's graphic environment? The grid will always be important to traditional graphic design, such as in printed books and magazines, but it has taken on a new life in the creation of websites and apps, especially as a method for unification over multiple viewing platforms such as computer screens and mobile devices.

The digital environment is constantly evolving, especially with the release of new devices, and the need to develop sustainable designs is paramount in creating a website that stands the test of time or at least five years. Gone are the days of flashy (or flash-based) websites that take a long time to load. The need for simplification and usability is crucial for a successful website, and this is enabled by grids. The most recent example of this is in responsive website design, where a grid is in defined as enabling a digital design to immediately transform depending on the screen configuration. This has led to a renewed understanding and overhaul of the grid that allows for semi-animated elements to thrive, thus proving that the grid is again at the heart of contemporary creativity.

PRODUCTION

D

B   V

Interview Matthew Lee **Photograph** Ivan Jones

BVD Design was founded by Catrin Vagnemark and Carin Blidholm Svensson in Stockholm in 1996. Rikard Ahlberg joined ten years later and is the company's third partner and design director. They work with numerous high-profile Swedish and non-Swedish clients such as H&M, Skandia, Ikea, Absolut Vodka, Coca-Cola and 7-Eleven. They also created the identity of the Design S, Sweden's national design award. We spoke to Rikard Ahlberg in BVD's studios in the Södermalm district of Stockholm.

BVD will celebrate its 20th birthday in 2016. What sort of company was it in the early days?
The company started when our creative directors Catrin Vagnemark and Carin Blidholm Svensson worked together. When I joined ten years ago there were seven of us, now we are 23. They worked with some great retail brands in the early days such as Ikea and H&M. I started at BVD on a freelance basis and was offered a position later.

What were the projects that helped shape BVD's identity?
We started off in retail, but today we also work in identity, packaging design, and strategy and innovation. An early project that combined all of our efforts was Apoteket Hjärtat, a Swedish pharmacy chain. We developed their complete graphic identity from scratch and have created packaging for around 500 products. They came to us with a blank slate, just their name.

When did you start using your motto, 'Simplify to Clarify'?
Over the last couple of years, together with our CEO Diana Uppman, we really tried to pinpoint and understand what we

do – and that is to simplify to clarify. It's what we've been doing all these years. Our philosophy is all about focusing on what's important and communicating clearly. We want to clear away everything that's unnecessary and find design solutions.

Is it important that your clients share this philosophy?
It is difficult to have a connection with a client if they don't believe in what we are trying to do. We are a business, not artists, and so we have a duty to solve clients' problems and we believe we can do that through our philosophy. There is a triangle of us, the client and the consumer, and all three must feel we have reached a good solution. We have a tried-and-tested process of working with clients. Dialogue is super-important to us and we think we're good at listening. There's never a 'ta-da' moment when we magically appear with a new logo. It's about working together with several possible options.

How can effective design enhance a client's brand identity?
Graphic design is a distillation of a brand's story. The logo is the heart of its graphic identity. We try to reach simple, clear design

solutions so our clients have graphic identities that will last 10 or 15 years without needing to be changed. Smart design should be durable and long lasting. When we think about sustainability, we need to create smart design that lasts.

Can you help reduce a client's environmental impact?

A while ago at BVD we questioned our very being. It was a time when globalization and the environment were on the agenda and we looked hard at what we do, which is to help companies sell more products. This means more packaging – and we asked if we should leave this business and do something else. A large part of the impact a product has on the environment is determined by the design process. We understood that we needed to use smart, sustainable design to help us reach a better place.

Is there a greater need for clear, simple design in a world in which we're spending more time online, receiving so many messages from so many places?

Yes, I think so. So many companies and brands are trying to reach you through online advertising, social media and so on. We need to calm everything down a bit. We need fewer products to choose from and clear messaging on the packaging so you can calmly make your choice.

On your Twitter account you say BVD Design makes brands 'continuously profitable'. Is there a clear connection between good design and commercial success?

We don't just do design for design's sake – we have a goal and that is to help our clients be successful. We have brand strategists on our team and they are an important part of what we do. For example, take Blossa, a Swedish brand of mulled wine – we started with nothing, created a concept and now it has 85% of the Swedish market. We did different-numbered editions each year and they sell like crazy. We used design as innovation to make it a success in the market.

Your work for 7-Eleven was highly acclaimed.

It's a fantastic project in the sense that we've had so much positive feedback from all over the world. I'm very proud that we were able to balance something very commercial – coffee cups for a major retail chain – with such a high-quality feel.

The horizontal line design differs over multiple formats (cups, bags, napkins, etc.). How did you create design rules to enable this flexibility?

The idea was to have the two line patterns meet out of step, creating the quirky feel that catches the eye, building the number seven. The two patterns are always in relation to each other but we scale them to get a pulse between different formats. An identity like this needs to be flexible and alive.

And you expanded the horizontal lines to create the stencil interface?

The lines in the 7-Eleven logotype were our inspiration for the identity as a whole, including the adjusted type with a stencil feel. The seven in the logo is built from two lines overlapping with a stencil space in between. We took that thought and brought it into the typeface.

Could this contemporary yet iconic design also work in the United States?

It was only for the Swedish market and so we designed it for Swedes. But, yes, I think it could work in the US. Functional design is often borderless.

Did it help 7-Eleven sell more coffee?

I haven't seen any numbers so I can't say.

Is there something typically Scandinavian about your focus on simplicity and clarity?

There probably is, but we're not following trends. We're just doing what we believe in. Maybe it's natural for us to think like this because of our Scandinavian heritage. I'm not sure.

Hasn't Swedish design long had an emphasis on functionalism?

I think so. For me, Swedish design goes back to the painter Carl Larsson who painted these fantastic images with Nordic light coming into the rooms. The Scandinavian style is about light and space. If people want to call BVD Scandinavian design that's fine, but I don't care so much about labels.

Does a preference for functional, unfussy design say anything about the kind of society you live in?

Maybe it does. We sometimes call Sweden a *mellanmjölk* – medium-fat milk – country. We also have full-fat and low-fat milk but in Sweden you're meant to be in the middle, not too full or too low. But simple design doesn't necessarily quietly fit into the middle. Simple design can be bold and aggressive too.

How did the Design S commission come about?

It's one we love to do because it's the most prominent design award in Sweden. We were working with Svensk Form, the Swedish Society of Crafts and Design, so I had some connections there. It started out in 2006 and we created the basic graphic identity – the symbol and the logo and so on – and we also got to make the physical award. It's an award for great designers – graphic designers, fashion designers, furniture designers, architects and so on – and so it's got to be top-notch, seriously sharp. It's also on a very small budget with very limited time. In this case, simplification was key. The S shape creates a very clear connection from the name of the awards and the logo to the award itself. A typographical solution that is simple and straight to the point seemed obvious. The identity of the award is absolutely clear. Every year we change the materials used and the production techniques. It always needs to feel valuable, like something you would be proud of winning, and it must always be made in Sweden.

What were the origins of the origami S?

We had already done Swedish wood and cast iron in the Swedish industrial tradition and so I was thinking about what we could do that's distinctive and Swedish. We have all this fantastic paper production in Sweden so I thought why not use paper to create the shape. And, of course, we're all fascinated by Japanese design and origami...

How many were produced?

Around 20, although it varies from year to year.

'A typographical solution that is simple and straight to the point seemed obvious. The identity of the award is absolutely clear. Every year we change the materials used and the production techniques. It always needs to feel valuable, like something you would be proud of winning, and it always must be made in Sweden.'

Who was the paper specialist you worked with on the 2014 S awards? How did your working relationship begin?

Egil Jansson is a talented friend of mine and he has done a lot of work with paper. I told him my thoughts and we found a way to build the S with the same proportions as the previous awards. We've never worked together before and we had a great time despite the time constraints. Egil is crazy in a good way.

Were there any technical issues in creating an origami S?

I originally wanted to create the S out of one piece of paper, but that wasn't possible, so it's actually made out of two pieces, folded and put together.

One of your Design S awards was made from Swedish wood. Does nature have an impact on your approach to design?

In Sweden we love being outside, close to nature, and we do lots of skiing and other sports. There's certainly something about that lifestyle that offers clarity.

Is there an extra pressure when you create something for your industry peers?

Of course. It's kind of crazy really.

What have you been working on with Coca-Cola?

We've been working directly with their global design office in Atlanta on their 'one brand' strategy, which will see the four types of cola marketed as a single brand. They understand the need to simplify to clarify and so we've been looking at getting rid of all the unnecessary design – the swooshes, the skeuomorphism – and going back to the 1970s when the ribbon was more prominent. We've been trying to get them to work horizontally rather than vertically on their cans. The script is so well known that even if you see a section of it you know what it is. We were invited to create posters for the 100th anniversary of the contour bottle, which incidentally was created by a Swede, Alexander Samuelson.

Do you enjoy these huge projects?

I do, although I worked on a series of business cards for a copywriter, a single individual, and I enjoyed it as much as any other project. It's all about solving a problem in a smart, clear way and that's what we live for.

Is the design world in general moving towards simplicity?

I think so, but maybe it will change. I don't think we'll ever change.

Carin Blidholm Svensson, Catrin Vagnemark and Rikard Ahlberg were photographed at the BVD studio in Stockholm, Sweden

BVD
DESIGN S AWARD

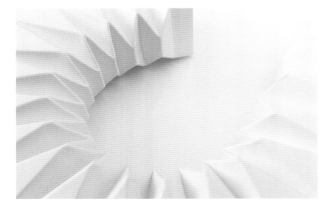

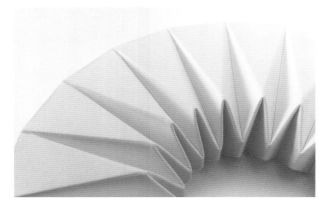

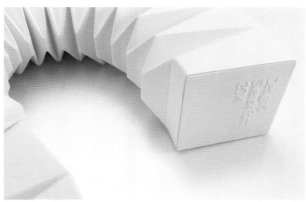

Design S is the leading design award in Sweden, which recognizes and celebrates excellence in design across all disciplines. Awarded each year by Svensk Form, the Swedish Society of Crafts and Design, winners in each category take home their very own three-dimensional S. Over the years it has been made from various materials, ranging from wood, metals and plastics to recycled computer screens. In 2014 Stockholm-based BVD, a strategic brand and graphic design agency, made it out of paper, creating a giant origami letter S.

The core value behind BVD is 'simplify to clarify'. The team value craftmanship and create designs that contribute towards social and economic sustainability.

Rikard Ahlberg, design director at BVD, explains that for Design S, 'The concept is flexible and unlimited, based on Swedish materials and production techniques.' The award was created out of Iggesund, Invercote G, which is Swedish paper from Swedish trees, specially produced for scoring.

Paper artist Egil Jansson crafted the award from just two sheets of Invercote G paper, using a score-and-die-cut technique and then folding, glueing and constructing the pieces together to form the strong, sculptural shape.

Publisher Swedish Society of Crafts and Design
Art Direction BVD
Design BVD, Egil Jansson
Production M-Print
Origin Sweden

STINSENSQUEEZE
PAPERWORK MAGAZINE

PaperWork is a self-published art writing magazine. It exists as a printed publication and as open events that accompany each issue, with contributors reading, performing and distributing their writing in a live setting. *PaperWork* is designed by Stinsensqueeze, a design studio with offices in London and Paris, and Ross Bennet. Each edition is printed on a risograph and loosely bound with a rubber band, then sealed in an envelope and embossed with the *PaperWork* logo. The envelopes are different for each issue; for Issue #1 *Lost and Found*, a metallic silver foil envelope was used and for Issue #2 *Act Natural*, a beige 95% opaque polythene.

Stina Gromark and Louise Naunton Morgan, design partners at Stinsensqueeze, explain, 'We use a loose binding method to allow *PaperWork* to be pulled apart and read in different ways. It can be performed, used like an object or a prop, or read as a collection. We used the envelopes because we wanted a cover that would function like a container for *PaperWork*, without a definite beginning or ending.'

Publisher PaperWork Press
Art Direction Stinsensqueeze
Design Stinsensqueeze, Ross Bennett
Production PaperWork Press
Origin UK

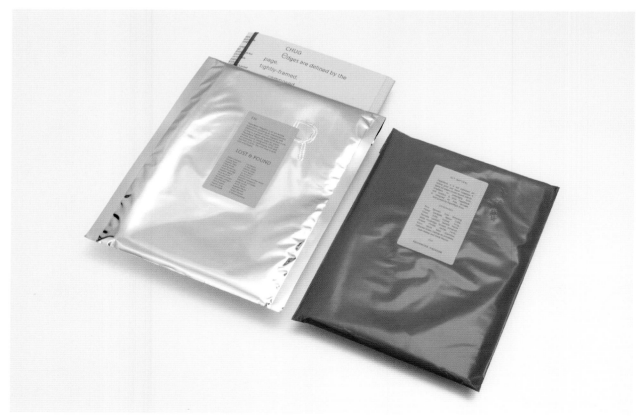

BEDOW
HANS ISAKSSON

A Title is a monograph on the work of Swedish artist Hans Isaksson. It was published to accompany 'Canvas', an exhibition of his work held in 2013 at Björkholmen Gallery in Stockholm. The bibliophile edition of 50 is signed and numbered, and has a shoelace as a bookmark, which refers to Isaksson's work *String*, an acrylic-on-canvas painting with shoelaces cut out from the canvas.

The book was designed by Bedow, a Stockholm design agency. Founder Perniclas Bedow talks about the work, 'the cover itself is an imitation of an artwork, with fake canvas material and specifications. Isaksson's works are not always what they seem to be.... We always try to be as quiet as possible when designing books for artists so we don't compete with their work. Instead, we try to find a good rhythm in the book, using different papers and printing techniques. And if you boil down Hans Isaksson's artistry to three things, you have copper, canvas and circles.' The cover is printed on a coated embossed paper that mimics canvas.

Publisher Björkholmen Gallery
Art Direction Perniclas Bedow
Design Sara Kaaman & Anders Bollman
Production Göteborgstryckeriet
Origin Sweden

Hans Isaksson
A Title, 2013
Ink and foil on paper
28 × 21 cm

HEY
JEREMY MAXWELL WINTREBERT

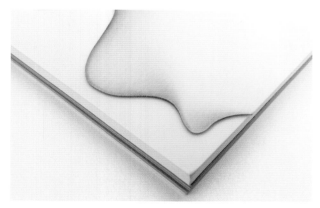

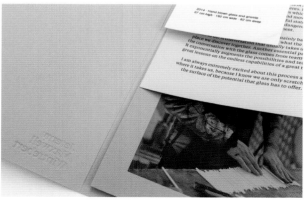

Jeremy Maxwell Wintrebert is a Paris-born glass artist who was raised on the west coast of Africa. At the age of 19 he discovered hot liquid glass, but until then painting was his main outlet. He also explored metals and clay.

Barcelona-based design studio Hey were appointed art directors of a print project celebrating Wintrebert's work and journey as an artist. As Verònica Fuerte, art director at Hey, explains, 'The starting point of the project was our wish to genuinely share what being a modern glassblower really means. We wondered how to communicate the spirit of the work beyond the formulaic pictures of the final artworks. Even though the works have to speak for themselves, unveiling the making is a way to complete their story and personality. Our aim is to share glimpses of the creative process and of the daily life within the workshop, adding special insights to what people would usually see through shows or pictures.'

The newly created visual identity translates this passion and the love of the process of glassblowing. Eva continues, 'We imagined the laser-burned pattern as a border for creativity. It also gives a hint of the intense heat inside the workshop. The burned paper even smells like the folded newsprint which is used as a tool to shape the hot glass.'

The final design, bound together using rubber bands to bring a burst of colour, is both a technical and conceptual reflection of the art of glass blowing.

Publisher Jeremy Maxwell Wintrebert
Art Direction Hey
Photography Roc Canals
Production Grafiko
Origin Spain

The Paper Book is the complete collection of creative papers developed and manufactured by Arjowiggins. The worldwide paper manufacturers state their intention boldly: this is the 'international standard for creative papers'.

There are no sections, dividers, illustrations or examples of usage, just hundreds of A4 pages labelled with a brief description of each paper stock. As Stephen Gilmore, partner at London-based creative agency North, explains, 'We aimed to make paper the hero, so that a user can experience a full sheet of the stock without being influenced by superfluous imagery. The aim was to create the ultimate reference tool – all a designer would need is a notebook and pen, computer, Pantone swatch and *The Paper Book*'.

Simple in its aim, the book itself was logistically complex to create. Rik van Leeuwen, from Eindhoven-based Lecturis, worked with three separate Netherlands-based binders on the project. 'There are 300 different types of papers, all needing to be in the right place, at the right moment, in the right order with the right text printed on it, on the right side of the paper. The key aspects of making this book were the dedication and communication between designer and printer, printer and binders and paper supplier, designer and printer.'

Publisher Arjowiggins
Art Direction & Design North
Production Lecturis (print), Makk (gathered), Patist (PUR binding), Abbringh (hardcase binding)
Origin France

MADE PUBLISHERS
PROCESS JOURNAL

Process Journal is a quarterly Australia- and USA-based graphic design publication art-directed by Made Publishers. The aim of the journal is not only to serve as a source of inspiration for designers, but also to take a look at the 'process' behind some of the world's most influential creative work. Printed on high-quality uncoated stocks, utilizing a five-colour printing process, the journal comprises 100 pages of advertising-free content.

For issue ten, *Process Journal* wanted to celebrate this milestone with the release of a bespoke typographic approach created exclusively by Triboro Design, based in Brooklyn. The cover was published in a standard and limited special edition, which was printed on an uncoated black stock with the 'New York' typography hot-foil-stamped in a gloss black foil.

As Thomas Williams, creative director at Made Publishers, says, 'We worked closely with Triboro and developed the bespoke "New York" typography to fit within the parameters for the cover format. The standard edition was specified with a "rainbow" foil, however, we also wanted to play with the contrast of coated and uncoated finishes on the black stock. Therefore, we also produced a limited number of the black-on-black covers that pay homage to the darker and grittier side of New York City.'

Publisher Made Publishers
Creative Direction & Design
Thomas Williams (Made Publishers)
Cover Typography Triboro Design
Production AZ Druck (Germany)
Origin Australia, USA

LANDOR
LESS

Less is the story of a wine lover who wanted to make good wine affordable for everyone, while minimizing its global impact. The idea was simple: remove the superfluous by inviting shoppers to fill their bottles directly from wooden casks stored in Cave Garibaldi's cellar in Saint-Ouen, France.

In keeping with the reduction of superfluous elements while maintaining minimal environmental impact, French brand consultants Landor created a design for the reusable bottles that ensured less packaging waste. This was achieved by working with local craftsmen with recycled materials and using ink pigments developed from wine to minimize sulfites. Design detail was sandblasted onto the glass bottle or added with die-cut labels.

As Tristan Macherel, creative director at Landor, explains, 'Removing the superfluous goes beyond aesthetics; *Less* is truly an eco-friendly wine. The brand reduced its carbon footprint by changing customer behaviour. When a bottle is reused, much less packaging goes to waste.'

Publisher Cave Garibaldi
Executive Creative Director Tristan Macherel
Copywriter, Namer & President Luc Speisser
Production Stéphane Quezel
Origin France

LESS

APPELLATION FRONSAC 2010
GRAND VIN DE BORDEAUX

LARS MÜLLER
ZAHA HADID ARCHITECTS/HEYDAR ALIYEV CENTER

Lars Müller, a graphic designer and educator, started publishing books on typography, design, art, photography and architecture in 1983. To coincide with the launch of the Heydar Aliyev Center in Baku, Azerbaijan, a book was published devoted to its construction, which was created by Zaha Hadid Architects.

The exterior shape and structure of the building was adapted for the minimal cover, which was pure blind embossed in three dimensions.

As Lars Müller says, 'Convincing Zaha Hadid Architects was easy. We all wanted to see the 3-D motive embossed, using high pressure, on the cover.'

The building is an open, inviting and curvilinear design, which is in strong contrast to the city's monumental Soviet-era architecture. Photographs display the building in all its facets.

Publisher Lars Müller Publishers
Art Direction Saffet Kaya Bekiroglu, Lars Müller
Photography Iwan Baan, Hélène Binet
Production Koesel GmbH
Origin Germany

DEUTSCHE & JAPANER
SIPGATE

When creating the editorial design for the annual review of Sipgate, a German telecommunications company, in 2013, graphic design studio Deutsche & Japaner wanted to focus on the personal and emotional aspects of the company rather than just the facts and figures which are normally associated with review documents.

To achieve this, Deutsche & Japaner created a typographic book cover printed using black hot foil, which references digital responsive design. The publication was then covered in screen-printed wrapping paper with personal quotations from employees, supporting a personal connection between the company and its staff who were surprised when they read their own words.

Publisher Sipgate GmbH
Art Direction & Design Deutsche & Japaner
Production Nino Druck
Origin Germany

6D-K
NT SFU:1

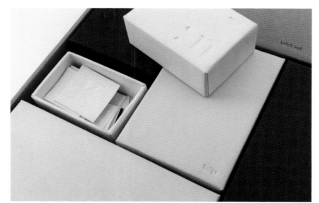

NT sfu:1 is a piece of promotional packaging design created for a unique textured paper range launched by the Takeo Paper Company. It has a soft non-slip texture similar to that of felt.

An important part of the initial design brief was to emphasize this unique texture and encourage people to hold and touch the paper, allowing potential clients to picture its infinite possibilities. The promotional tool was art-directed by Shogo Kishino, from Japan-based studio 6D-K: when you pick up the box it reveals a number of individual delicate boxes, each containing a small surprise interactive gift, which encourages people to engage with the product.

As Kishino explains, 'Opening a sharp, edgy box will create friction, as the paper gets rubbed together, but inside are smaller boxes with goods such as puzzle pieces and envelopes which are neatly packed together in a grid influenced by the silver ratio.'

Art Direction Shogo Kishino (6D-K)
Design Shogo Kishino, Miho Sakaki, Nozomi Tagami
Production 6D-K
Origin Japan

A3 STUDIO
SERVICE DE LA CULTURE DE LA VILLE DE LAUSANNE

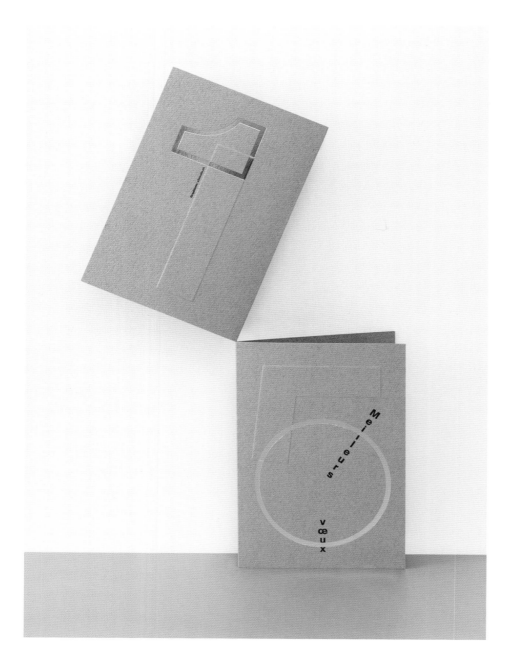

For their 2015 greetings card, the City of Lausanne's Department of Culture commissioned local graphic design agency A3 Studio to create their own interpretation of the traditional format.

The beautifully produced card draws on a minimalist design aesthetic and geometric figures, which, when assembled, represent the digits 1 and 5 of the new year. These simple shapes are printed using different techniques, ranging from embossing, letter-pressing and foil stamping, which are a high contrast to the natural blue fibres of the uncoated paper.

The result is a non-traditional reinterpretation of the yearly festival that is enhanced with a subtle combination of design and print production, making the card a collectible object.

Art Direction Yvo Hählen,
Priscilla Balmer (A3 Studio)
Design Yvo Hählen
Production Atelier Typo de la Cité
Origin Switzerland

PRODUCTION

DARREN WALL
SEGA MEGA DRIVE/GENESIS: COLLECTED WORKS

Aiming to be the definitive retrospective of the iconic videogame console, this cloth-bound book, folio and slipcase features development and concept illustrations for Sega's best-loved game franchises, as well as original developer interviews and previously unseen hardware production plans.

Creator Darren Wall says, 'Up until the Sega Mega Drive was launched at the end of the 1980s, consumers were used to videogame consoles being

utilitarian grey or cream boxes. The Mega Drive deliberately borrowed its style from high-end audio equipment. To echo this for our book, we used a high-gloss ink screened onto a heavy-duty acrylic-coated cloth. The small red dot represents the power light on the console, a dramatic touch suggested by illustrator Kam Tang.'

Publisher Read-Only Memory
Art Direction & Design Darren Wall
Illustration Kam Tang
Production Daniel Mason, Graphicom, K2 Screen
Origin UK

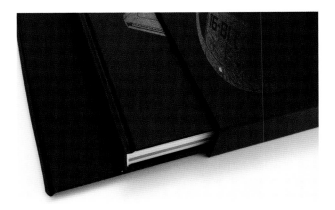

KASPER-FLORIO
MISSUE

Swiss electro duo Missue describe their release 8K as 'a concept album based on the 14 highest mountains on our planet. Their summits are on the one hand closely connected to the planet and on the other to the interface of heaven and the magical unknown. The mountains are both beautiful and dangerous at the same time. Owing to the power of their own magnetic and physical radiance, mountains are intuitively seen as holy. Mankind is made to feel humbled and transient in the presence of the stony expanse.' Kasper-Florio are a design studio based in St Gallen, Switzerland, founded by Larissa Kasper and Rosario Florio. They were commissioned to create a limited-edition version of Missue's first ever physical release. They created

a 3D landscape mould with black pigments. 'We wanted to create a physical object that differs from the digital release and makes it worthwhile to buy a CD, in times when most of the audience might not even have a CD player anymore. The artwork is supposed to be a monumental artefact derived from the musical concept.'

The cover design wilfully omits the title and the name of the artists. Florio continues, 'The idea was to create a mysterious scenery to complement Missue's soundscape. We gave the information content as low a profile as possible.'

Publisher Reframe Records
Art Direction & Design Kasper-Florio
Production Tamara Cattozzo, Andrea Rüeger (casting), Lehner Druck (embossing)
Origin Switzerland

JASON RAMIREZ
THE CORPSE EXHIBITION

The Corpse Exhibition is a collection of short stories by Hassan Blasim that relate to the Iraq War from an Iraqi perspective, creating a portrait of a country and a people in the throes of war. The monochrome cover is a stark approach that designer Jason Ramirez, under art direction from Penguin Books USA's Paul Buckley, thinks 'convincingly captures the author's unique world, better than a photographic treatment of war-torn Iraq or her fallen peoples'.

'Reflecting upon the stories and the war, I kept returning to the number of Iraqi lives lost throughout the conflict', Ramirez continues. 'I decided to pursue a pure typographic treatment. The aim: to transform the cover into a stark and gritty landscape that might represent the raw terrain explored through these stories.'

'Given that the stories are macabre, it seemed appropriate that the cover should be printed in black. The blind deboss of the type – set in a large point size with ample letter and line spacing to cover the entire field of black – represents the immense loss of life, as well as graves dug to bury the corpses.' The application of a gritty matte finish, along with the blind deboss, provides a tactile component to the cover which reinforces the pitfalls of wartime Iraq.

Publisher Penguin Books USA
Art Direction Paul Buckley
Design Jason Ramirez
Production Coral Graphic Services, Inc.
Origin USA

NEUBAU
NEUBAU FORST CATALOGUE

Neubau are a graphic and typographic studio founded by Berlin-based designer Stefan Gandl. The studio create contemporary, modernist-inspired design and a number of resource books containing vectorized everyday objects and natural environments.

Neubau Forst is the follow-up book to *Neubau Welt* (2005), a catalogue resource consisting of everyday objects illustrated as vectors (it was also published by Lars Müller). This new edition features numerous trees systematically photographed in summer and winter over several years in their Berlin surroundings, which have been redrawn as detailed vector graphics to be used as a resource by graphic designers. The resulting body of work is incredibly detailed, unlike other vector tree resources that use the Adobe Illustrator autotrace tool.

The grey linen and debossed book-cover design also display the NBF-Locator-Grid system, a minimalist sequence of dots that pinpoint, when placed over a city map, the location of the 72 documented tree locations in the city of Berlin. The first pages of the book unveil all this reference information in layers of the NBF-Locator-Grid reference.

Publisher Lars Müller Publishers
Art Direction Stefan Gandl (Neubau)
Design Stefan Gandl, Benjamin Ganz
Photography Benjamin Ganz, Stefan Gandl, Akane Sakai, Daniel Cottis, François Lehérissier, David Pope, Lukas Reinhard
Illustration Benjamin Ganz, Stefan Gandl
Production Kösel, Altusried-Krugzell
Origin Germany

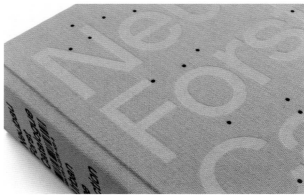

HORT
CITY BY LANDSCAPE

City by Landscape, published by Switzerland-based Birkhäuser Verlag, documents the work of Rainer Schmidt Landschafts-architekten + Stadtplaner. They are German landscape architects whose work explores the interface between urban planning, open-space planning and architecture. The company's overriding objective is to find answers to the urban-planning problems of today, and to do so in the awareness that 21st-century landscape architecture should be a 'built' reflection on how people deal with one another and with nature.

A series of essays and 40 of Rainer Schmidt's pivotal case-study projects (including the Business Towers in Munich, the park city in Schwabing, the Doha Exhibition Centre and the Great Mosque of Algiers), along with project statements, are included within a series of six books.

The individual books, designed by the German graphic design studio Hort, are systematically arranged to reflect the large spectrum of diverse works by Rainer Schmidt without categorizing them in a traditional format. The cover is typography-only, black-on-grey, and printed on uncoated paper stock with a flash of colour on the edges. Each volume increases in size and the typography consistently rises a point size to the same ratio. The result is a very puristic and consistent kind of book design.

Publisher Birkhäuser Verlag GmbH
Art Direction & Design Hort
Production Druck & Verlag Kettler GmbH, Bönen/Westfalen
Origin Germany

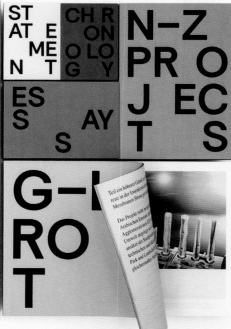

A FUTURE WITHOUT
WILL PLOWMAN

Will Plowman, musician and co-founder of the record label A Future Without, creates music that is about capturing a certain moment in time and his own personal reflection on that moment and space. This project captures four piano improvisations, in four different locations, and uses a variety of recording techniques to mould the works into fully finished compositions. For Plowman, 'The sonics and atmosphere of the environments become as important as the piano itself.'

Plowman wanted the packaging to 'reflect the simplicity and delicate intricacy of the music'. This led to the production of an origami sleeve for the 10" vinyl. 'It came about from discussions about what physical products mean in a digital age. Using origami gave a new beauty to our sleeve designs and a tactile involvement with the consumer.'

Art Direction Will Plowman,
Ross Tones (A Future Without)
Design Will Plowman
Production Squared Roots
Origin UK

Swiss filmmaker Orsola Valenti captured six films of Cindy Van Acker's solo dance performances. The Belgian dancer and choreographer always blurs the boundaries between dance, performance and the visual arts. Paris-based studio Akatre were asked to create a package that matched the choreographer's unconventional approach.

The creators Valentin Abad, Julien Dhivert and Sebastien Riveron describe how the box is 'delicate visually but rough to the touch. The work of Cindy can seem rough but it's really masterful. We tried to translate this feeling with a rough paperstock.' Other surprises come from a juxtaposition of black-and-white photography with vivid red and blue DVDs and gleaming hot-stamped foil type. Debossed type, on Curious Matter paper, inserts muted tones and completes this tactile treat.

Publisher Cie Greffe, Cindy Van Acker
Art Direction & Design Valentin Abad, Julien Dhivert, Sebastien Riveron (Akatre)
Production Imprimerie du Marais
Origin Switzerland

TREVOR JACKSON
FORMAT

In the age of digital music downloads and music streaming sites, popular for convenience rather than personal connection, few predicted the meteoric rise of traditional music formats such as the vinyl record and even the cassette tape. The collectability of tangible releases has afforded graphic designers the opportunity to experiment visually – and with innovative production techniques.

In 2015, UK creative director and musician Trevor Jackson released FORMAT, a 12-track album featuring new music compositions, his first release in 14 years. Each of the 12 tracks has been released individually on different, and sometimes previously obsolete, music formats including vinyl records (7", 10" and 12"), CD, mini-CD, cassette, USB, VHS, MiniDisc, DAT, 8-track and reel-to-reel. Each track is available individually, in limited editions (from just ten reel-to-reel tapes to 500 12" singles), depending on the format, or collected in the Vinyl Factory Edition boxed set, which houses each release in a white corrugated plastic box with individual formats sunk into position in each layer of the tray.

Publisher The Vinyl Factory
Art Direction & Design Trevor Jackson, The Vinyl Factory
Production The Vinyl Factory
Origin UK

TREVOR JACKSON / FORMAT

COLLECTED EDITION

12" VINYL / 10" VINYL / 7" VINYL / CD
MINICD / CASSETTE / USB / VHS / MINIDISC
DAT / 8 TRACK / REEL TO REEL
EDITION OF 10 + 3 AP
P+C TREVOR JACKSON 2015
THE VINYL FACTORY
VF116-12

MARK VIDLER
AKKORD HTH020/HTH030

Akkord, the reclusive electronic music collective from Manchester in the UK, create elemental music shaped by a passion for maths and sacred geometry. Their HTH020 EP, released by Houndstooth, an independent record label, is influenced by experimental sound design, old school jungle and modern bass music. The HTH030 release features remixes by acclaimed underground electronic artists The Haxan Cloak and Vatican Shadow. As Leo Belchetz from Houndstooth says, 'The colour scheme is reversed in every element. The colour of the vinyl on HTH020 was grey, with a plain black label, whereas HTH030 includes traditional black vinyl, with a plain grey label. The design concept is a reflection of the music, which is stripped back, dark and foreboding.'

Publisher Houndstooth
Art Direction Akkord
Design Mark Vidler
Production Key Production, Optimal Media, MPO, The Delga Group
Origin UK

BOB DESIGN
BUBU

The Bubu Spectrum, published by Bubu, is a compendium of swatch books that showcase the range of specialist print finishes and binding techniques offered by the Switzerland-based book-binding specialists. This is the second compendium in the series, designed by BOB Design, who are based in London and Zurich. The books are uniformly bound and titled in white, a colour specifically chosen so the array of unique print and binding qualities on show are placed centre stage.

As Mireille Burkhardt, founding partner of BOB Design, explains, 'The books are bound and titled only "white on white" to make the haptic qualities of each explicitly visible and comparable. The books are meant to be used as "swatches" for designers to establish the perfect binding technique for a project.' The list of print production techniques on show is staggering, including thread-stitching, relief-deboss, emboss, deboss, silk-screened, laser-cut, engraved, UV-varnish, flockage, rounded spines, fabric jacket, visible binding and acrylic tape, all housed in a fluorescent red perspex case.

Art Direction Mireille Burkhardt & Kieran O'Connor (BOB Design)
Design Aaron Merrigan (BOB Design)
Production Bubu
Origin Switzerland

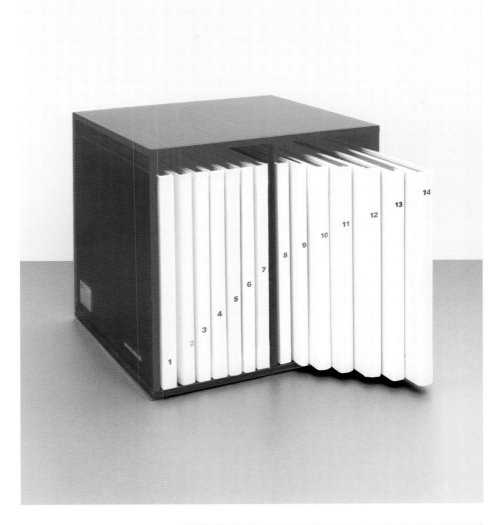

BROWNS
RELIGIOUS SYMBOLS/LONDON GARDEN BIRDS/
NUMBERS/SEXUAL PREDATORS/POLITICAL SYMBOLS

Designed by Browns and published by Browns Editions, founding partner Jonathan Ellery's most recent publication consists of five books, each with different subject matter. Below the colourful covers unfolds a curious, absurd and sometimes dark narrative. Each book takes us on a journey of sorts, as strange frictional relationships appear. Ellery presents these interweaving complexities in a minimal, direct and honest way within five foiled, cloth-bound books, each with a screen-printed coloured gel cover, housed in a signed, white screen-printed box edition of 150.

A single element from within each book was placed on the cover and reinforced with a strong colour to create an unusual relationship between the five publications. The oddities on the covers are only the surface of a more complex and sometimes dark narrative that starts to unfold. Unlikely neighbours, and the frictions they create, tend to be what Ellery's work is all about. His clarity of thought and the concise arrangement of his ideas resonate through all areas of his art practice. He playfully works across a wide range of media from sculpture to performance, film to photography. The medium of book art is also central to his work, and he moulds paper, fonts and images as he would any other medium, to create tactile, hand-numbered art objects.

Publisher Browns Editions
Art Direction & Design Jonathan Ellery, Sateen Panagiotopoulou (Browns)
Production Pureprint Group
Origin UK

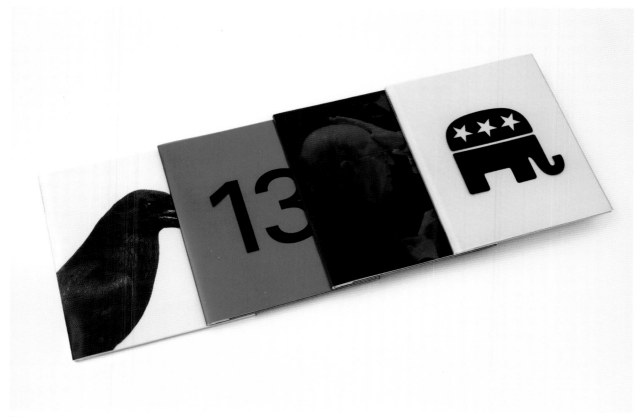

Religious Symbols
London Garden Birds
Numbers
Sexual Predators
Political Symbols

Ellery

CONDIVISA
FEDRIGONI

When launching the Sirio Ultra Black paper range, Italian paper manufacturer Fedrigoni wanted to publish a promotional booklet to showcase the print production potential of this blackest of black papers. The ultra black is black 28, the deepest and most intense of all the 28 possible shades of black.

The swatch book, designed by Italian graphic design studio Condivisa, presents the range of ultra black paper weights with a series of print techniques such as embossing and hot-foil stamping alongside bold fluorescent typographic designs. This is the only reference to ornamentation, along with die-cut windows and laser engraving. The resulting book is a deep black simple design where the emphasis is on the paper and the production.

Publisher Fedrigoni Spa
Art Direction & Design Condivisa
Production Studio Fasoli
Origin Italy

115 g/m²

115 g/m², E/R 65 Fiandra

185 g/m²

280 g/m²

370 g/m²

ERMOLAEV BUREAU
SEVERNEFTEGAZPROM

Severneftegazprom, one of the largest oil-gas-condensate fields in Russia's Far North, commissioned the Moscow-based design studio Ermolaev Bureau to refine their visual identity. As Vlad Ermolaev, founder of Ermolaev Bureau, explains, 'One of the main points of the creative brief was to keep the initial shape of the logotype and company's colours.'

Three basic geometric graphic elements became central to the design, representing the company's three main activities:

point, field and exploration; point could be compared with a point on a map. Hand-fed and turned by Cliché Letterpress in Novodmitrovskaya, cylinders from Korrex Nurnberg presses, manufactured in Germany between 1910 and the 1970s, were turned over blocks to deboss the geometric design onto a range of stationery and book covers.

Publisher Severneftegazprom
Art Direction & Design Vlad Ermolaev (Ermolaev Bureau)
Production Cliché Letterpress, Megapolis
Origin Russia

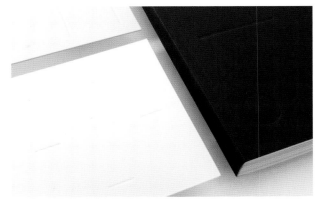

OLAF BENDER
RASTER-NOTON

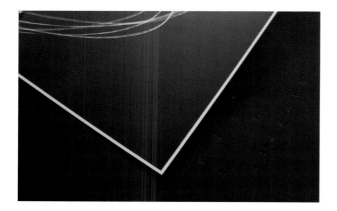

Raster-Noton is an experimental electronic music and art network based in Chemnitz, Germany. It was founded in 1996 by Olaf Bender and Frank Bretschneider and in 1999 it merged with noton.archiv für ton und nichtton, founded by Carsten Nicolai, to create raster-noton (archiv für ton und nichtton).

Since then Raster-Noton has published music and art, blending the boundaries between pop, art and science. The common idea behind all releases is an experimental approach, an amalgamation of sound, art and design, which is not only apparent in the music, but also visible in the minimalist cover design, often realized in monotone and type-only cover artwork.

Full album projects, such as Kangding Ray's 'Solens Arc' and Emptyset's 'Recur', are released in limited-edition vinyl records, characterized by minimalistic black scored cardboard packaging and debossed typographic title details created by label owner Olaf Bender. Each release is accompanied by a limited-edition photographic print signed by the musician, which is a large-scale replica of the standard release cover. This attention to production creates a collectible series that reflects the experimental, minimalist nature of the music.

Publisher Raster Noton
Art Direction & Design Olaf Bender
Photography David Letellier
Production Druckerei Gröer, Richter Kartonagen
Origin Germany

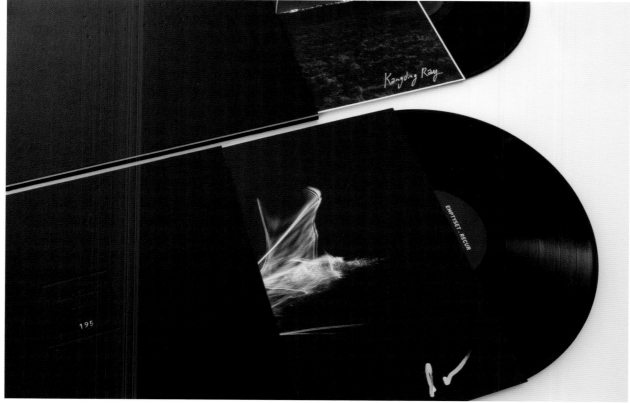

DALSTON CREATIVE
SEE THE LIGHT

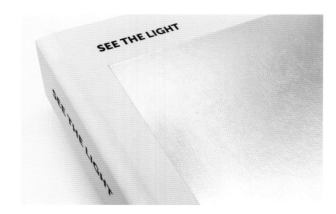

See the Light, published by Arvinius + Orfeus Publishing, is an inspirational book that showcases the work of Swedish light designer Svante Pettersson.

Pettersson's perception of light is that it keeps changing how it affects material objects, depending on location and environment. To realize this concept, Swedish graphic design studio Dalston Creative were commissioned to art-direct the book. As Sofia Darke explains, 'We wanted to mimic Pettersson's idea of light and create a cover that gives the viewer an experience of something changing.'

The resulting cover incorporated a holographic foil, embossed onto the front, a beautifully simple device that changes depending on the light and on the angle you hold it.

Author Svante Pettersson
Publisher Arvinius + Orfeus Publishing
Art Direction & Design Magnus Darke, Sofia Darke (Dalston Creative)
Production Livonia Print
Origin Sweden

IZET SHESHIVARI
PIERRE SCHWERZMANN

Pierre Schwerzmann is an artist who lives on the shores of Lake Geneva in Switzerland. His approach to minimalist painting aims to go beyond the boundaries of what is visible on the canvas by merging space with the surface of his paintings.

In publishing Schwerzmann's work, Boabooks broke with the traditional format of a book in favour of different-sized pages to generate strong iconographic and rhythmic ellipses.

The thread-sewn book was released with four different colours printed on multi-layered silkscreen on a rough cardboard with a special ink. By contrast, the inside pages reveal a perfectly smooth surface by using a selective raster printing process. Stochastic screening is used for the black printing and a fine 100-LPI mechanical screening is used for the colour with the aim of perfecting the gradient and reproducing the detail of the movement of the artist's brush, from a three-metre-wide painting to each single page of the book.

Publisher Boabooks
Art Direction Izet Sheshivari
Design Pierre Schwerzmann, Izet Sheshivari, Olivier Weber
Production scan graphic, Nyon (lithography), Courvoisier-Attinger SA, Bienne (printing), Timotei Keller, Geneva (cover printing), Buchbinderei Burkhardt, Mönchaltorf (binding)
Origin Switzerland

DEUTSCHE & JAPANER
IMPRIMERIE DU MARAIS

Imprimerie du Marais, a Parisian printing house, showcase their expertise in paper and printing techniques with the work of talented and prestigious design studios. In 2014, to produce *Notebook II*, they turned to the German creative studio Deutsche & Japaner to create an entire visual identity for their calling-card project. The creative team commissioned eight prominent graphic design studios from across the world to each create a notebook.

The project relies upon a plethora of production techniques to give each notebook its unique character, including foiling, textured embossing, micro-embossing, gold foiling, multi-level embossing and sewn bindings. It is driven by one of Imprimerie du Marais's maxims: 'the print becomes the object'.

It is housed in a natural kraft box, which once opened reveals the vast array of design and production techniques, allowing them to take centre stage.

These techniques are a dying art form, and the project is a tribute to them.

Publisher Imprimerie du Marais
Art Direction Deutsche & Japaner
Design Adriaan Mellegers, Anagrama, Bureau Mirko Borsche, Homework, Ouwn, Partel Oliva, Present Perfect, Research and Development
Production Imprimerie du Marais
Origin France

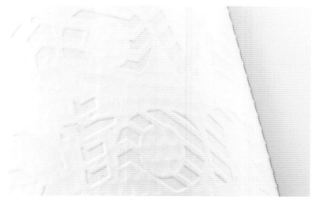

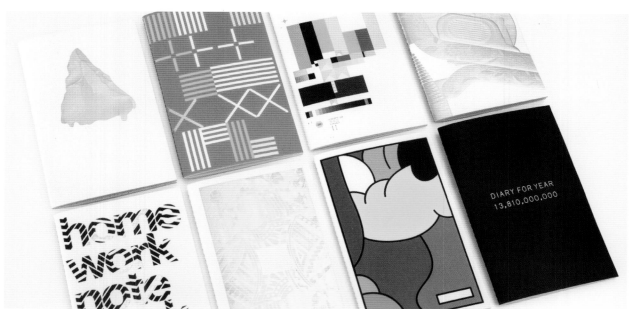

Designs by

Anagrams
Bureau Mirko Borsche
Homework
Olive Partel
Ouwn
Present Perfect
Research and Development
Studio Adriaan Mellegers

un imprimeur: huit designers

Edited by
Imprimerie du Marais,
Paris

MUCHO
DESIGN HUB

The *Prestige Book* is a printed record of the conception and construction of the Design Hub building in the Barcelona Design Centre. It was created by Oriol Bohiga's MBM Arquitectes.

The publishers, Spain-based Acciona/Copcisa, commissioned Mucho, a global graphic design partnership, to create a publication that emphasizes the building's orientation and multi-layered connectivity through its neighbourhoods, employees, districts, disciplines and cultural and technological areas.

To achieve the concept of connectivity, Mucho designed a unique cover and page-opening mechanism. Each turn of the page reveals unique configurations of the title typography, which on the fifth page uses silver foil and embossing.

The opening pages, and the journey through each page layer, act as connectors that reveal different forms derived from Oriol Bohiga's MBM Arquitectes' original construction plans designed to generate 'windows' that connect each space.

Publisher Acciona/Copcisa
Art Direction & Design Mucho
Production Sprint Copy
Origin Spain

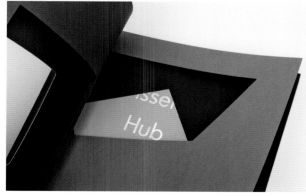

PENTAGRAM
NICK CAVE

The Sick Bag Song, published by Edinburgh-based Canongate Books, chronicles the Australian musician Nick Cave's 2014 tour of North America with his band, The Bad Seeds. This account of his 22-city journey began life scribbled on airline sick bags and grew into a restless full-length epic, seeking out the roots of inspiration, love and meaning.

The book's pared-back aesthetic takes inspiration from the object itself: the pristine and functional sick bag.

This simplicity, combined with white, red and blue foiling, and blind embossing, creates a cover that is both sterile and tactile.

Set within a clamshell box, the unlimited edition of *The Sick Bag Song* echoes the easy elegance of corporate America, politely contrasting with the visceral writing within.

Publisher Canongate Books
Art Direction Angus Hyland (Pentagram)
Design Charlotte Retief, Rhian Edwards
Production L.E.G.O. S.p.A.
Origin UK

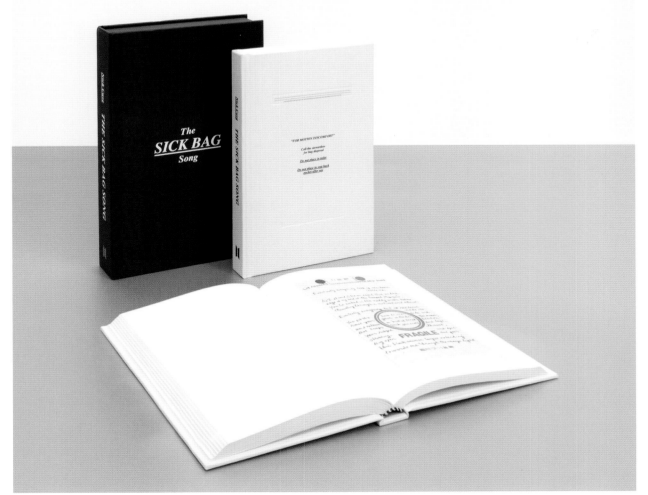

PAPERLUX
GMUND URBAN

Gmund are a German specialist paper manufacturer with over 180 years' experience. For the Gmund Urban collection, they partnered with German fine paper manufacturer Römerturm to create a highly textured series of stocks that is a homage to all urban centres around the world: warm, dusty colours nestle up against surfaces of cement, wood and graph paper.

To help promote the Urban collection, Gmund commissioned Paperlux, the German design studio and print production specialist, to create a unique packaging box inspired by urbanity. In the words of Max Kuehne, creative director at Paperlux, 'The basic concept of the design is the element of the line, which links all design disciplines in the modern living space – regardless of whether we speak of architecture, interior design or product design.'

These interlocking grid lines, realized through a series of hot foils and screen prints, cross over the die-cut sample boxes,

including a Hakoya Box made in Japan, which are held together in a slipcase. This also serves as the cover of a drawer. Inside each of the boxes are the original material inspirations, wood and cement, alongside samples from the entire Urban paper collection.

The colour scheme for the outer boxes is deliberately monochrome, referencing modernist building structures, but with accented copper-coloured hot foil. Headline and title type was set in Neuzeit Grotesk, with the addition of a specially drawn lowercase 'r'.

The result is a dream project for any print-design studio and utilizes state-of-the-art materials to create our idea of urbanity through a working promotional package. Kuehne continues, 'We consider this tool an invitation to the recipient to design his own personal urbanity; to continue the line, pursue perspectives and connections.'

Art Direction Max Kuehne, Daniela Gilsdorf (Paperlux)
Production Paperlux, Printarena, Ermonis, POP Werbeteam, Florian Böer, HEMA Druck
Origin Germany

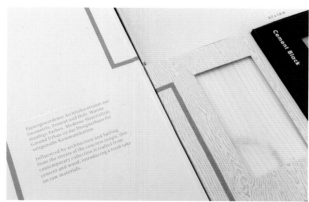

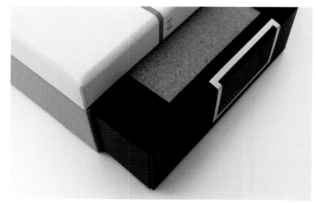

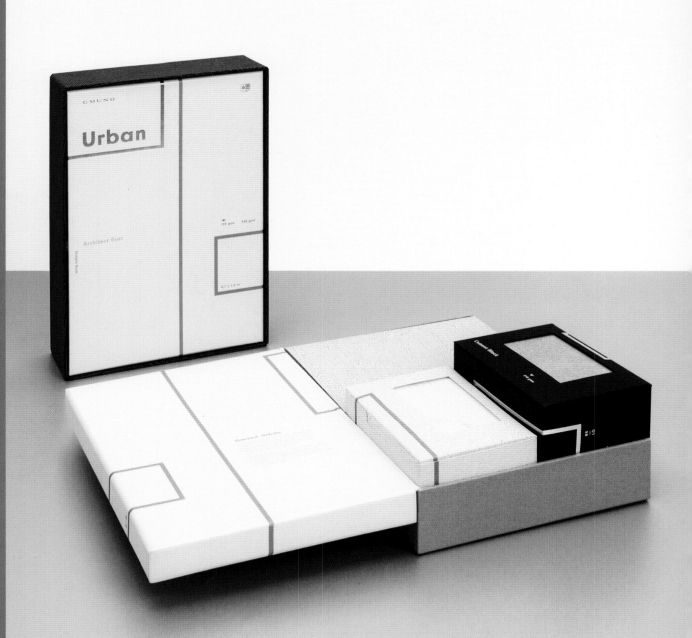

HAW-LIN SERVICES
PB 0110

PB 0110 are a fine bags and natural leather fashion label based in Hanover. Their philosophy, defined by founder Philipp Bree, is centred around how natural materials, such as vegetable-tanned natural leather, pure linen and brass, change with daily use and become even more beautiful over time.

Their design collateral for product launches and promotions, developed by Berlin-based design studio Haw-lin Services, underlines PB 0110's commitment to minimalist design and the importance of fine materials. The launch invitation to the company's first collection, with typography printed using blind embossing on board and a virgin natural leather slipcase, reflects the core philosophy of seeing the bag as a beloved object, a blank canvas that is developed and nurtured by the owner.

Publisher PB 0110
Art Direction & Design Nathan Cowen, Jacob Klein (Haw-lin Services)
Production Gutenberg Beuys Feindruckerei
Origin Germany

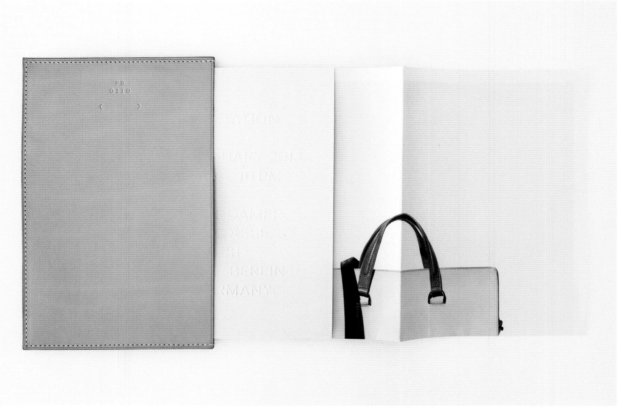

MATTEO COLELLA
STUDIO MARONATI-CASNIGHI

To promote their plastic surgery practice, Italian Studio Maronati-Casnighi commissioned art director Matteo Colella to create collateral that is centred around Maronati-Casnighi's belief that a diamond is a metaphor for their profession. A diamond, and the association of cutting to reveal beauty hiding behind an imperfect appearance, provided the inspiration for the promotion of Studio Maronati-Casnighi. The studio pride themselves on making people feel beautiful.

A pure black-and-white approach was preferable, so as not to contaminate the design with colour. The diamond concept was utilized with a series of chopped headline letters which feature throughout. Along the edges of these cut letterforms are scored folds that allow the poster to be folded into an information brochure format.

As Colella explains, 'In the beginning the users receive a folded brochure with a famous Italian proverb on the front: "Molti individui, come i diamanti grezzi, nascondono splendide qualità dietro una ruvida apparenza" which translates as "Many individuals, as rough diamonds, hiding behind a splendid rough appearance".' This underlines the connection between people and diamonds.

Art Direction & Design Matteo Colella
Production Unigrafica Srl Milano
Origin Italy

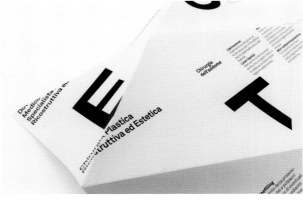

HAROON MIRZA
FACTORY FLOOR VS HAROON MIRZA

The Vinyl Factory, an independent music and arts label based in London, publish specialist artist and musician collaborations pressed onto vinyl records using their century-old plant formerly owned by EMI Records.

Created in conjunction with Haroon Mirza, this vinyl record was released to coincide with the artist's 2013 exhibition, entitled /o/o/o/o/, at the Lisson Gallery in London. The exhibition and subsequent record reflect Mirza's experiments with the interplay and friction between sound and light waves and electric current, and were cut directly onto 180-gsm vinyl lacquers by The Vinyl Factory.

This hand-signed release, in a limited edition of 100, also features a remix by the post-industrial band Factory Floor and is in a custom-made copper-foiled high-gloss black outer sleeve. With a front cover designed by Mirza, the artwork encapsulates the materials and processes used by the artist to create his sound samples. Mirza explains, 'I often use copper tape on or scratch into smooth materials such as perspex or glass in order to play them on a turntable like a record. The cover is a reference to the materials I use to create sounds that feature in my work. The gold-foil block references copper tape and the subtle white line refers to a scratch on a vinyl record.'

Publisher The Vinyl Factory
Art Direction Haroon Mirza, The Vinyl Factory
Design Haroon Mirza
Origin UK
Production The Vinyl Factory

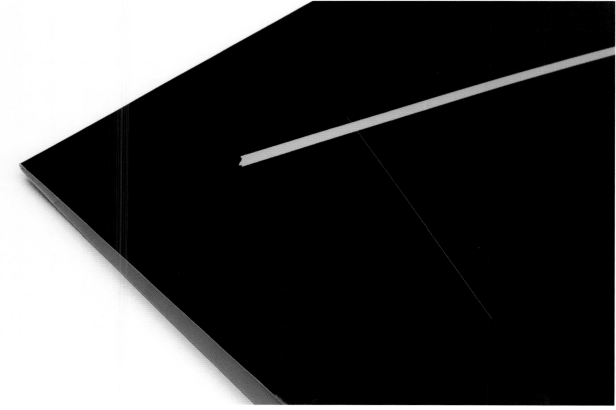

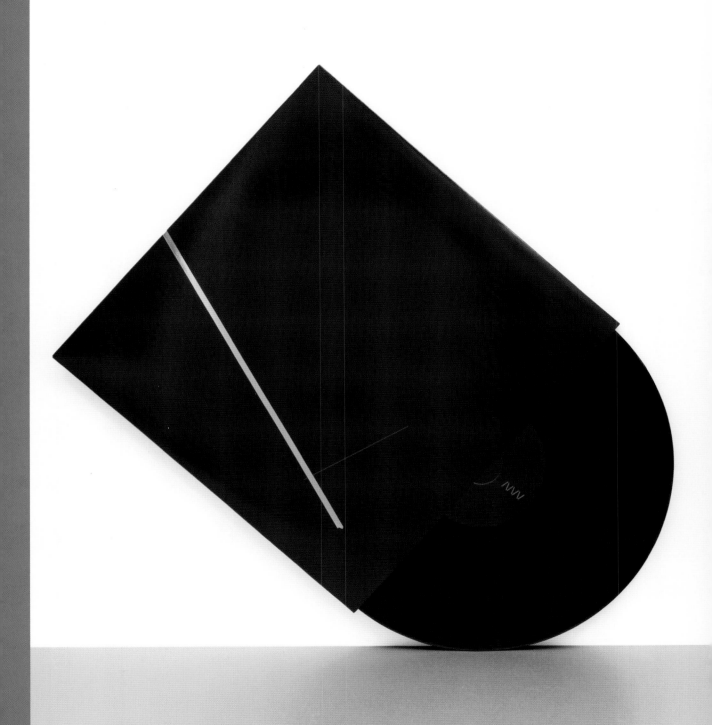

PAUL SCHOEMAKER
NICHTSDESTOTROTZ

'Nichtsdestotrotz' means 'nevertheless' and is a collection of short stories in magazine format by German publisher and graphic designer Paul Schoemaker. It includes works by Andreas Steinbrecher, Jan Vismann and Charles Bukowski, as well as plenty of self-made illustrations.

Schoemaker marries the brevity of the stories with the essence of a magazine: 'short stories are so easily read. You can read them in a lunch break or on a short train ride – that's why the magazine is a very handy format.'

The simply designed and self-published magazine makes a bold, creative move – each cover is torn. For Schoemaker, 'the act of tearing apart the cover is a short story itself. It makes a strong statement but at the same time it leaves a lot of room for interpretations – just like a good piece of literature.'

Publisher Paul Schoemaker
Art Direction & Design Paul Schoemaker
Production Digitale Druckkultur Düsseldorf
Origin Germany

FELD
ERASED TAPES COLLECTION V

To celebrate their fifth anniversary, Erased Tapes Records, a UK-based independent record label featuring contemporary classical music composers, wanted to create a limited and collectible release.

The label worked closely with the Berlin-based FELD design studio to create a hand-crafted box set, limited to an edition of 500. The box is made from heavy, high-quality card that has been dyed black, manually debossed and folded to resonate with the minimalist, raw sound of the music pressed onto 5 x 7" vinyl records. As Robert Raths, founder of Erased Tapes Records, explains, 'Seeing the label was home to ten artists at the time, it seemed logical to compile an album of ten exclusive songs – one per artist. The 7" format was chosen as it naturally groups the collection into five discs, labelled with big Roman numbers – one for each year.' This allows each composition enough space to stand on its own, while the logo-shaped record centre acts as the link between all artists.

Publisher Erased Tapes Records
Art Direction Torsten Posselt (FELD), Robert Raths, Sofia Ilyas
Design Torsten Posselt (FELD)
Illustration Chris Hernandez, Herr Müller, Torsten Posselt
Production The Vinyl Factory, Maren Thomsen
Origin UK, Germany

ESTUDIO EDUARDO DEL FRAILE
EXTENSO

Extenso is an exceptional wine, produced in a limited edition of only 600 bottles by the Spanish winery Carchelo Wines. As the name suggests, Extenso is designed to be shared over a prolonged period by a group of people celebrating a special occasion. The winery nurture long-working relationships, especially with specialist oenologists, to create a distinctive wine bottled in 1.5 litre bottles, which are designed to be shared.

The limited-edition bottle and lightweight wooden box were created by art director Eduardo del Fraile, founder of Estudio Eduardo del Fraile, a Spanish packaging-design specialist agency renowned for their innovative use of materials and print-production techniques.

To enhance the exceptional quality of the wine, each bottle was screen-printed and hand-painted to create a minimalist yet personalized design. As Fraile explains, 'The idea was to focus on its forms, highlighting them in order to emphasize geometry rather than the brand itself. The key to synthesis is to establish an information hierarchy. In this case, the form of the product goes before the brand; consequently, the product becomes more iconic and distinguished. I think that when you work this way, the design transcends and makes the life of the product longer.'

Publisher Carchelo Wines, Spain
Art Direction Eduardo del Fraile
Design Estudio Eduardo del Fraile
Production Valldeperas
Origin Spain

EXTENSO

STUDIOMAKGILL
SPECIALS APPLIED

Specials Applied is a series of promotional booklets created for an independent British paper manufacturer, G . F Smith. The first two booklets, in an on-going series, are the first time a curated showcase for five different paper stocks from the company's specialist range has been published. The booklets, targeted at graphic design professionals and printers, aim to highlight specific applications or particular services that each paper stock offers.

As Hamish Makgill, founder of StudioMakgill, a Brighton-based studio, puts it, 'The main objective was to make sure the paper and the processes do all the communicating and not to detract with busy graphics.'

Publisher G . F Smith
Art Direction & Design StudioMakgill
Production Benwells
Origin UK

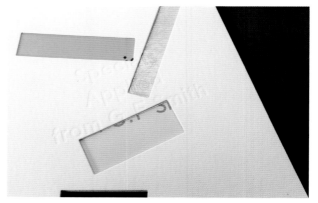

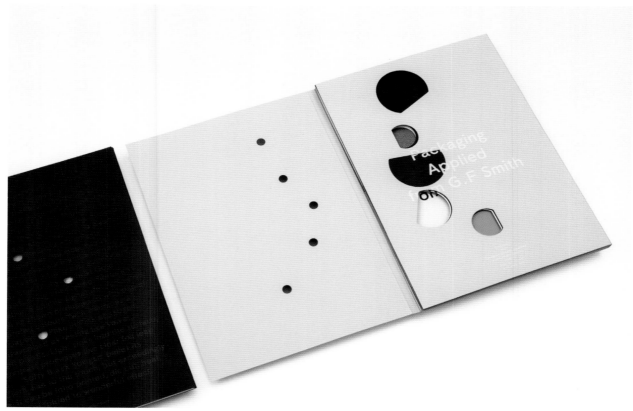

WANG ZHI-HONG
YOHJI YAMAMOTO

Making Clothes is a collection of autobiographical essays by Yohji Yamamoto, the world-renowned Japanese fashion designer whose tailoring for men and women is often based upon oversized silhouettes in black, with drapery and textured elements.

Taiwanese graphic designer Wang Zhi-Hong reflects upon his response to the design brief, 'Yohji Yamamoto's designs are renowned for use of fabrics and his tailoring skills. I made a conscious effort in the use of the materials throughout the book to reflect his craftsmanship – screen printing, embossing, a thread-sewn book block with black thread and an exposed spine. For paper, I opted for NT Rasha Shikkoku paper from Takeo Paper in Japan.

'Black is Yohji Yamamoto's signature colour, so I used extra-black paper. The thread-sewn binding approach exposes the black thread on the spine, hinting at the connection with fabric.'

Publisher Faces Publications
Art Direction & Design Wang Zhi-Hong
Production Younger Print
Origin Taiwan

ALEXANDER BROWN
AMON TOBIN

Amon Tobin, a Brazilian electronic music producer, has been releasing epic, futuristic music with Ninja Tune, a UK-based record label, since 1997.

Dark Jovian, which was released as a Record Store Day exclusive on the yearly event date of 18 April, is a completely white, multi-material vinyl release which encapsulates Tobin's fascination with sci-fi. Two 180-gsm vinyl records are housed in a white silicone 'wheel' scored on each side. One includes the five original recorded tracks while the reverse features an audacious non-playable 2-D etching. The etched sides of the two vinyl discs face outwards, creating a protection for the audio groove side.

The release is a perfect realization of Tobin's exploratory music. Creative director Alexander Brown explains, 'Amon's music has an epic, cinematic feel – so I think the music and the artwork can feel very coherent. The artwork is more artefact than anything, using the physical textures of the materials to create a more sculptural artwork.... I always had in mind not the avid fan, but the uninitiated – someone curious enough to find it lurking in someone's record collection, and it will hopefully feel minimalist, enigmatic and intriguing.'

Publisher Ninja Tune, Just Isn't Music
Creative Direction Alexander Brown, Amon Tobin, Sean Preston
Design Alexander Brown
Production Antoine Dube, MPO France, Mpack
Origin UK

SAVVY STUDIO
HÅNDVÆRK

Established in New York, Håndværk is a lifestyle brand founded by husband and wife team Esteban Saba and Petra Brichnacova. It specializes in the manufacture of clean, minimalist clothing, using the finest natural materials combined with craftsmanship. Each item is handmade or hand-finished in collaboration with other family-owned workshops, which share their commitment to producing garments of exceptional quality.

To communicate Håndværk's minimalist brand approach and high-quality production, creative director Petra Brichnacova draws from her experience as a textile and surface designer to create graphic design that is inspired by nature's authentic beauty. She works closely with Savvy Studio, a brand communication agency based in Mexico, to realize these ideas through clean, crisp packaging that combines uncoated paper stocks with embossed surface details. The result is a carefully considered, premium approach that emphasizes Håndværk's commitment to craft. As Brichnacova explains, 'We do not want anything to take away from the quality of the materials and the details in our products. The simple packaging and minimalist design are meant not to garner attention, but to complement our overall aesthetic and the handmade nature of the products.'

Art Direction Rafael Prieto, Bernardo Dominguez (Savvy), Petra Brichnacova (Håndværk)
Production r-pac International Corp.
Origin USA

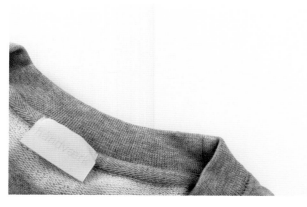

BVD
COCA-COLA

To celebrate 100 years of the iconic contour bottle, Coca-Cola Global Design invited 100 leading graphic designers and studios renowned for their simplified graphic approach to create an original poster inspired by the shape of the glass bottle created in 1916. The 'Coca-Cola Bottle: An American Icon at 100' campaign features all of the 100 designs, alongside original artwork by Andy Warhol, exhibited at the High Museum of Art in Atlanta, the town that provided inspiration for the drink's famous original secret recipe.

BVD, a Swedish strategic brand and graphic design agency, established a working relationship with Coca-Cola (see the interview on pages 112–15) and took inspiration from the fizzy drink bubbles and words associated with the iconic brand to create a bright red, minimalist poster. The resulting artwork is a die-cut poster that reveals the shape of the iconic bottle when each of the text bubbles is removed. As Rikard Ahlberg, partner at BVD, explains, 'Bubbles are an obvious shape to use when it comes to communicating the brand. We wanted the exhibition visitor to interact with the poster, perhaps choosing one of the 100 bubbles, reading the word in it and thinking about it.'

Publisher Coca-Cola Global Design
Art Direction & Design BVD
Production Coca-Cola Global Design
Origin Sweden

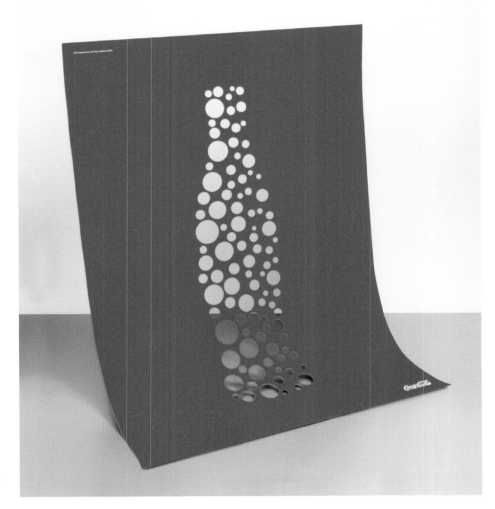

DEMIAN CONRAD DESIGN STUDIO
ART BASEL

Art Basel, based in the Swiss city of Basel, is a premium contemporary art fair founded by the resident gallerists Bruckner, Hilt and Beyeler in 1970. Today, the yearly art fair has morphed into a global event with fairs in Basel, Miami and Hong Kong.

The brief for promoting the 2014 event, art-directed by Lausanne-based Demian Conrad Design Studio, was to create something new and fresh for the Swiss campaign. Demian Conrad presented initial design concepts that deviated far from the main corporate guidelines. In Conrad's words, 'The most difficult part was to deal with two heritages, first the rebranded concept from the global agency Interbrand and second the clever previous visual identity created by graphic design studio Müller+Hess.'

The fair has always had a simplified approach and the studio found inspiration through the 'super normal' discipline coined by designers Morrison and Fukasawa.

Minimalism needs to be constructed over several layers, and the designs reflect a contemporary art fair in an abstract manner, which is rare in a global arena where emphasis is placed on standing out. These designs acquire an extra special value because of the simplified design and print production. Conrad continues, 'Marc Spiegler, the Art Basel director, is a big fan of the WROP (water random offset printing) technique we invented and we wanted the printing production to acquire a kind of cool and authentic factor that we are missing among millions of cheap digitally printed material.'

The campaign was printed in several formats; the posters were screen-printed, half with a fully automatic printer and the other half with a semi-automatic one, with the surface being covered with as much ink as possible.

Publisher Art Basel
Art Direction & Design Demian Conrad Design Studio
Production Uldry SA
Origin Switzerland

Art | Basel

Basel | June | 19 – 22 | 2014

 UBS

ALEC SOTH
PING PONG

Alec Soth, an American photographer, is a partner in the Magnum Photography collective and founder of Little Brown Mushroom Books.

For several years, Soth has combined his passion for table tennis and photography by collecting vernacular 'ping pong' photographs. For his book, *Ping Pong*, published by Little Brown Mushroom Books, Soth asked Geoff Dyer and Pico Iyer, writers and fellow table-tennis enthusiasts, to respond to these collected images by engaging in a metaphorical literary ping-pong match to accompany selected images.

For the cover, Soth enlisted the help of graphic designer Hans Seeger who transformed the traditional cover template into a bespoke ping-pong table, which appears when the front and back cover boards are opened up. This simple action, accompanied by the net design on the spine, creates a fun, image-less cover that perfectly reflects the content.

Publisher Little Brown Mushroom Books
Art Direction Alec Soth, Pico Iyer, Geoff Dyer
Design Hans Seeger
Production The Fox Company
Origin USA

MUCHO
INTERNATIONAL TRUCKS & TRACTORS

ITT 1878 is a luxury edition hardback book that tells the story of International Trucks & Tractors, a machinery distribution company based in Spain, France and Morocco with a 130-year history.

Art-directed by Mucho, a graphic design partnership with offices around the globe, the publication recounts the company's history. The minimally designed metal cover is made from white-coated anodized aluminium and includes metal embossing and black silk-screen printing to emphasize the company's history in mechanics.

As Marc Catalá, creative partner at Mucho, explains, 'The book is about a machinery distribution company, so they basically deal in trucks and tractors, that kind of thing. We needed something on the cover that would make the book a precious object while still conveying the brand's values of strength and boldness. Having metallic covers in the fashion of a truck or a tractor's hood made sense.'

The result is a typographic cover that emphasizes the core values of the company while remaining simple but beautiful.

Publisher ITT International Trucks & Tractors
Art Direction & Design Mucho
Illustration Ibrahim Yogurtcu
Production Leicrom
Origin Spain

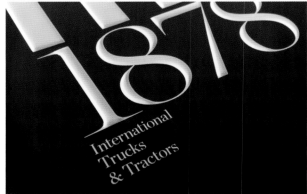

THE DESIGNERS REPUBLIC
APHEX TWIN

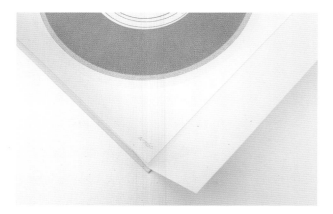

Syro, the first full album to be released by UK electronic music pioneer Richard James, aka Aphex Twin, since 2001, was launched after the teaser appearance of a blimp featuring the Aphex Twin logo, which floated over London, and stencil graffiti in New York.

The album was available in the standard digital, CD and vinyl releases, and a deluxe limited-edition vinyl box set. It featured original artwork by Sheffield-based The Designers Republic, who have a long-standing relationship with Aphex Twin. In their typically playful style, The Designers Republic worked closely with Aphex Twin on the artwork to create a design that documents every cost involved in the production of the album – a detailed list ranges from technical equipment and promotion through to postal expenses.

The pinnacle release was the hand-crafted deluxe limited-edition vinyl box set, created in close collaboration with James Burton from Warp Records. Presented in an acrylic slipcase and limited to an edition of 200, it is the most collectable of all the formats. The production list also became central to this design, appearing over gatefolds and vinyl sleeves, and the deluxe edition was accompanied by a bonus intaglio print which was hand-printed and presented in a case-bound print folio.

Publisher Warp Records
Art Direction The Designers Republic, Richard James
Design The Designers Republic
Production James Burton, Neil Woodall (Intaglio Printing)
Origin UK

APHEX TWIN
SYRO

minipops 67 [source field mix]	120 2
XMAS_EVET10 [thanaton3 mix]	120
prndm 29	10
4 bit 9d api+e+6	125 26
180db_	
CIRCLONT6A [syrobonkus mix]	141 98
fz pseudotimestretch+e+3	125
CIRCLONT14 [shrymoming mix]	134 85
syro u473t8+e [piezoluminescence mix]	152 97
aisatsana [102]	141 98
s950tx16wasr10 [earth portal mix]	165 97

Watermarked CD promos	£0 00118
finished copy CDs for sync promotion	£0 00073
Customs copy	£0 04007
Journalist travel expenses	
from France to London	£0 00133
UK press day expenses for Leah	£0 00391
UK shop-visiting and promotions in US	£0 00001
500mm × 500mm square floor sticker	£0 00425
Venue hire for LA listening party	£0 01215
tesills placements and promotions	£0 00406
tile tracking pre lean and monitored	
the costs of album download	£0 01519
Lunch for Leah and UK journalist	£0 00002
Postage costs to UK radio station	
and travel to UK radio station	£0 00134
Room hire for Warp album playback	£0 00091
at screening rooms	£0 00098
Postage costs for UK radio promotion mailout	£0 00035
Online advertising in Norway	£0 02215
CD 8s for UK radio promotion	
Production of short Aphex Twin logo films	£0 00041
Postage costs for radio promo	£0 0001
Postage costs for radio promo	
mailout in Germany	£0 00099
Pay-per-click retail advertising in US	£0 00095
Online advertising in Spain	£0 00133
Postering in Copenhagen and Aarhus	£0 00006
Printed press release for Japan	£0 00166
design and print	£0 00004
Digitisation from tape archive copy of	£0 01325
The Making of Windowlicker	
Window posters in Dublin, Ireland	£0 0009
Social media advertising in US	£0 00232
Production cost for	£0 0310
retail clear folder for Japan	
Print advertising in UK	£0 00283
James's expenses for press pass	£0 00407
Postering in cafés in Sydney	£0 00041
Melbourne and Brisbane	
Online advertising for planning meeting	£0 00196
Dinner and refreshments in Germany	£0 00028
press promotion mailout in Japan	£0 00075
Venue hire for Montreal listening party	£0 00122
A1 retail poster for Japan	£0 00106
Taxis and lunch's expenses for	£0 00024
meetings and lunches with writers	£0 00057
Venue hire for NYC listening party	£0 00729
A2 retail posters	£0 00224
Lacquer processing second cut A/B/C/D/E/F	
including test pressings	£0 00094
Refreshments and lunch for promo team	£0 0004l
Acetate listening party in Melbourne	£0 00052
Retail laminates for retail in Australia	£0 00122
Printing of posters for retail displays and	£0 00142
café poster run in Australia	
Outdoor postering in Brussels	£0 00009
Acetate pressings	£0 01988
Digital video network advertising in UK	£0 01426
Retail marketing and racking in Australia	£0 00291
James's flight to Berlin for press pass	£0 00021
Production cost for retail poster for Japan	£0 00042
Website bandwidth costs	£0 00027
Test pressings outsourced to Richard	£0 00041
Online advertising in Denmark	£0 00099
Refreshments for LA listening party	£0 00099
Billboards in Japan	£0 02355
Independent Invoice racking	
and promotions in US	£0 00577
Production cost for retail	
logo magnet for Japan	£0 00177
Watermarked CDs for sync promo mailout	£0 00289
Retail marketing and racking in Belgium	£0 00282
Promotion and marketing team in Denmark	£0 00166
key's expenses for meeting with pressing plant	£0 00005
London sync promotion campaign	£0 00406

EXCESS MEETS LESS

America in the 1950s was a world away from bankrupt, post-Second World War Europe. Production and consumerism were king and a new visual language was developed to feed this excess. It was during this time that a radical new visual direction based on minimalism was developed.

By Simon Kirkham

Consumerism doesn't get the phrase 'you can't have your cake and eat it'. Why ever not? It thinks cakes are made to be eaten.

In 1950s America, having felt the crisis of the Great Depression and a fierce Second World War, Americans were all for having an extra dollop of ice cream on their Knickerbocker Glories. Holding back and saving the dollars wasn't the order of the day – the spirit was 'live for the now' and the promise was 'you can have it all'. Consumerism was in full swing: cue fast foods and fast cars. It was time for Dunkin' Donuts (1950), KFC (1952), Frozen T.V. Dinners (1953), Burger King and McDonalds (1954). And in the car lot, Oldsmobile Futuramic (1950), Cadillac Series 62 (1952), Pontiac Chieftain (1953) and Chevrolet Bel Air (1954).

Although Pepsi (1965) didn't use the term 'max' until the early 1990s, 'max' was certainly the mindset of the 1950s and early 1960s. Everyone simply had to have everything. Eat your cake, buy another cake. We all get richer in the process. By 1960, one sixth of working Americans were employed directly or indirectly by the automotive industry. The decade was its golden age, inventions and innovations in air-conditioning, automatic transmission, power-steering, power brakes, seat-belts and the V-8 engine making mass production viable. The car industry turned the United States into an economic powerhouse. The big three were General Motors, Ford and Chrysler, and they enjoyed international sales. Huge family cars set about advertising their many features. In press ads this meant cramming everything onto a single page, because the convention at the time was the more you throw at something, the more likely something will stick. A 1951 Ford ad ran with the headline 'Built for the years ahead – with 45 "look ahead" features', which it then went on to list. And the 1953 Pontiac 4 DR stated, 'No car so good ever cost so little', but like so many ads of the time it never sought to substantiate the claim in any way. In fact, such ads made so many assertions that it was apparent advertisers felt all they needed to do was tell a driver their car was the best and they would want to buy it. There were two common traits: a raft of features and a raft of over-claims. What was the regular man (and it was always the man when it came to car-buying) supposed to think?

The visual styling of 1950s automotive press ads can best be described as a slalom of features that meander through the page, distracting the eye at every turn along the way. This approach was given credence by a sociological theory at the time – 'Maslow's Hierarchy of Needs', a pyramid that read (from the bottom up): 'physiological', 'safety', 'love/belonging', 'esteem' and, at its pinnacle, 'self-actualization'. Maslow said that the basic-level needs must be met before an individual would strongly desire any of the above. In short, filter this into advertising and you've got 'always say the lot': an all-bases-covered approach, so that the man (let's call him Joe, which was the most common name) would hold onto at least one fact that might become his opinion, giving him a bragging right when defending his

'You see, the creative mavericks who were around at the time were also pushing back against something far more malignant and insidious than cramming things in. They were seeking to change a profession that told out-and-out lies.'

purchase. It all added up to a lot of Joes all saying they had the best car.

But what if your brief fails even to register on the bigger and better scale? What if no amount of telling could convince people, because, clearly, the car was small, bug-like and designed by Hitler?

Before we get to the oft-seen Volkswagen Beetle ads, it's worth a mention that the more considered ad makers began to realize that research groups, where products were discussed at length with a cross-section of the target audience, weren't necessarily the best basis on which to construct an ad. Tried and tested, yes; but writers were pressured to write about every benefit discussed, hence the industry sticking to the Maslow hierarchy that created clutter on the page.

There were ad men who thought differently, notably Leo Burnett, David Ogilvy and Bill Bernbach. They each headed up agencies that formed the opinion it was better to sell one strong message than confuse with many. Nowadays, many agencies that stretch back this far claim retrospective involvement with this clear mode of thought. Quotations from the era still abound on agency websites today. The Volkswagen Beetle ads created so much cut-through with their simple, minimalist approach

that it ignited a 'creative revolution' – to use the ad-industry term for what happened. The campaign came from an agency called Doyle Dane Bernbach (DDB). Not only did it apparently 'define the 1960s for baby boomers as much as rock 'n' roll did' (*Adweek*, 2011), being heralded as the 'Greatest Advertising Campaign of the Century' (*Ad Age*, 1999), but it also did something truly groundbreaking for those outside the industry. It told the truth.

You see, the creative mavericks who were around at the time were also pushing back against something far more malignant and insidious than cramming things in. They were seeking to transform a profession that told out-and-out lies. As Leo Burnett stated, 'Regardless of the moral issue, dishonesty in advertising has proved very unprofitable.' And as David Ogilvy pointed out to his team, 'You wouldn't tell lies to your own wife. Don't tell them to mine.'

The problem was the clients themselves, who were proffering the lies which were then simply copied verbatim and embellished with an overstatement or two – this was the creative sparkle, the expectation of what advertising was in those days. Copywriters weren't termed copywriters at this point. They were called writers, and they had no art-director partner – the standard process was to put the 'story' into the design department. Clearly, dictation governed content and integrity was lacking.

Despite having the nutritional content of cardboard, a leading cereal came up with the headline 'Protein!' and cigarette companies were running rampant with claims such as 'More doctors smoke Camels!' and 'Pleasure helps your disposition. It's a psychological fact!' The abundance of exclamation marks in ads prior to Volkswagen did, at least, easily allow people to spot the disingenuous.

Youth culture became increasingly suspicious of anyone older than themselves. Jack Weinberg, informal leader of the free-speech movement that swept California in 1964, famously said, 'Don't trust anyone over thirty.'

The conditions were perfect for minimalist ads to achieve cut-through. And with minimalism came an intrinsic link to a new and refreshing honesty.

The Volkswagen Beetle 'Think Small' ad was the first minimalist advert to break the mould. It featured white space – glorious White Space, deserving its capitalization. It might seem odd to refer to nothingness as a feature, but White Space is a term used routinely in advertising practice. Designers appreciate its ability to help direct the eye. The 'Think Small' ad was the cause of such talk; never before had advertisers considered not filling the page. The image of the Volkswagen Beetle, small and not even centred, invites the viewer to peer into the scene. Yes, a scene.

The shadow of the undercarriage puts it on an imagined road, and the quarter-left positioning leads you to think it is being driven towards you, as if introducing itself. Even if unconsciously, the viewer does make these connections, and easily decodes the ad without any brain strain whatsoever. Conversely, too much imagery – as with garishly crammed, stretched car ads complete with picket fences, horse paddocks, picnics, children, dogs, engine cutaways and so on, often causes viewers to look away. The brain says there is too much to take in, and if the content is hyperbole bordering on lies then it's a hard sell for the average Joe to stomach. It's like being shouted at, whereas 'Think Small' speaks normally.

The minimalist context ascribed to the ad is, of course, a product of hindsight. The ad wasn't intended to set out a minimalist manifesto, although that's a bandwagon advertisers are happy to jump on. Yes, the car was small, but it didn't have to be small on the page. The creators accentuated its diminutiveness for effect. Interestingly, when reading that 1950s Volkswagen advertising 'broke the mould', there is an artistic subtext given to it, as if it wilfully defined a 'movement'.

Today we are more likely to accept that advertising is not art, despite Andy Warhol and his like. These are the words of Bernbach in 1949, writing his 'creative revolution' manifesto: 'Let us prove to the world that good taste, good art, good writing can be good selling.' It's as if he's not simply expressing the voice of brands, but setting up to

'If the idea was small (but actually big and groundbreaking) then the execution was minimalist. So how much of its enduring appeal was simply down to design?'

subvert art into advertising. This is an ad man being great at his job – selling. He says as much. The 'revolution' is a piece of internal thought leadership: the context is advertising. It's all too easy to be swept up in this and attribute minimalism to the cause. A design aesthetic is one thing, advertising is another; for one, it has a job to do. In this case the concept was small, hence the execution was small. The brief governed the solution. The tone needed to be refreshingly honest, because the Volkswagen Beetle was a sitting duck otherwise. You simply couldn't lead with anything other than an acknowledgment of what you're seeing – a small car. It's like when comedians walk out on stage: they're nearly always self-effacing about what it is their image conveys. So much so that 'I know what you're thinking…' has become a ubiquitous opening line. An audience likes to know that you're aware of who you are and also of what they are thinking. It's a trust thing. The same is true of ads. Hitler's 'Volks Wagen' or 'people's car' was designed to evoke German nationalism – this was certainly an opening gambit worth steering clear of. 'Small', and the benefits thereof, was the better option in the face of cars becoming crazy-big. Deciding on this

point of difference led to the minimalist approach, not the other way round. Put simply, 'Think Small' was the best solution to the brief.

The ad's humbleness belied its cleverness as a sales tactic. It still made the consumer feel superior by appealing to a certain kind of snobbery – to those consumers who felt themselves to be a cut above, not in terms of 'more and more', but 'less is more'. The Volkswagen Beetle was for those who saw through the 'bigger is better' mantra, for those who felt impervious to the advertisers' guile. In short, the ads made the consumer feel smug – exactly the same result hoped for with the ads that preceded it.

And it smashed it in terms of sales. The Volkswagen Beetle went on to outsell huge car dealers such as Cadillac and General Motors. It's also the reason you probably didn't recognize the names of their cars mentioned at the start of this essay. The Beetle eclipsed them all and has gone from strength to strength ever since. When others ground to a production halt, the Beetle kept trundling on, without needing to stop for petrol – just as it had promised in the 'Think Small' body copy. In 1963, sales surpassed one million, up from the 150,601 sold in 1958, just one year before the 'Think Small' campaign. This was simply astonishing – an unprecedented marketing success. But to put all this down to minimalism would be misleading.

If the idea was small (but actually big and groundbreaking), then the execution was minimalist. So how much of its enduring appeal was simply down to design?

Futura type played a supporting role. It is a simple, unembellished sans-serif typeface that metes out clarity. As an interesting aside, it wasn't until 2004 that American road signage came round to sans-serif type, because it was proved to be more legible. The instigators of this change, Don Meeker and James Montalbano, cited Volkswagen ads when convincing the road authorities to make the switch.

The page layout throughout the campaign pleased the eye, too. A tray of copy along the base of the page is still a treasured and trusted device used for print communications. It literally creates a visual foundation, one that the ad can be built and ordered around. The positioning of the Volkswagen logo, though not exactly bottom right, is also de rigueur. In fact, housing it to the left of the third column makes it look modern by today's standards, where the tendency is lazily to plonk the logo in the far bottom right. The three-column rule established by Volkswagen ads suited its refreshingly short and punchy sales copy – copy that cajoles through the build-up of assurance and persuasion.

It's repetitive, too, like a poem. The clipped, precise nature conveys a reasonable argument, not the gushing, wordy, superlative-laden prose that came before. In both, 'Think Small' and the subsequent ad 'Lemon', you won't find one exclamation mark.

When you look at the broader brushstrokes of its influence, 'Think Small' might just have easily been termed 'Think Different' – Apple's minimalist advertising in the 1990s, which surely drew direct inspiration from Volkswagen. Apple consciously adopted minimalism, once White Space had meaning. Furthermore, Steve Jobs was a well-known minimalist by principle. You couldn't have said this of Bill Bernbach, who would have created artistic clutter had the brief demanded it.

Bernbach would have happily agreed, though he also knew the value of a story. 'Think Small' was followed up by 'Lemon', which furthered the notion of truth being bound to minimalism. Like 'Think Small', it was written by Julian Koenig and art-directed by Helmut Krone. It was produced under the tutelage of Bernbach, who actually devised the notion of a creative team – a copywriter plus an art director who are jointly responsible for the ad. This teamwork created a dynamic new rigour – the creative team went to the factory to interview the workers on the production line.

As the story goes, the task of Kurt Kroner, an assembly – plant inspector, was to flag up unacceptable marks on a chrome strip across the glove compartment. He had the power to reject any given vehicle on a scratch basis. He said these blemishes made the car a 'Lemon'. This became the breakthrough headline. For an auto brand to call their car a lemon had pure shock value, not least because it was (and still is) shaped like one.

The copy includes the line, 'This preoccupation with detail means the VW lasts longer and requires less maintenance, by and large, than other cars.' And in this neat turnaround we have the powerful sell. The ad ends with the words, 'We pluck the lemons, you get the plums.'

It's a great example of the principle 'The truth is in the product – you need to go and find it.' The one-word headline was a truly minimalist statement.

Hundreds of ads within this campaign followed suit: truth governed the concept and minimalism dictated the execution, although you could say minimalism ran through them, because the concepts were so simple. Either way, the formula worked. Every perceived slight was smoothed and rounded, ending on a positive sell. Here are a few of the headlines and snippets of connecting copy that concluded on a positive note.

1962: And if you run out of gas it's easy to push.
A figure of 32 miles to the gallon can make you a little hazy about when you last filled up.
1964: It makes your house look bigger.

You can buy a new house for who-knows-how-much?
Or a Volkswagen for $1,675.
1965: Presenting America's Slowest Fastback.
The VW engine may not be the fastest but it is among the most advanced. It's made of magnesium alloy…

When the message is to be believed – as the Volkswagen ads were – devices such as abundant White Space, sans-serif type, generous line spacing, a thin supporting copy tray, etc., are all in attendance. It's easy to say truth and minimalism cannot be separated. When honesty is laid bare, the best way to illustrate it is surely via a minimalist aesthetic. These design cues conspire to persuade us of the ad's honesty and integrity. They've set a tone for advertising ever since. The appearance of truth is the most valuable commodity that design can lend to advertising.

However, not all Volkswagen ads in this set stand the test of time. One of the ads from the same much-loved campaign is blatantly sexist, with a headline (a long one) that reads: 'Sooner or later your wife will drive home one of the best reasons for owning a Volkswagen' (the image shows the front wing smashed in).

The benefit: 'VW parts are easy to replace.' Yet the design integrity is the same as 'Think Small' and 'Lemon'.

It's perhaps churlish to insist that only some of the Volkswagen ads merit the tag of minimalist, but it is undoubtedly the case. One that makes the cut depicts

'Advertising, more than any other visual medium, begs, borrows and steals. It evolves by optimizing its message. And, of course, it builds on its previous successes. These elements can be boiled down in part and applied to the new.'

a simple curved line representing the bonnet, roof and boot. It reads: How much longer can we hand you this line? (1965).

As the ads progressed through the 1980s, another one for the Volkswagen Beetle Cabriolet stands out as being minimalist without even mentioning the product truth. It was so brutally simple it only showed an enlargement of the logo with its top sliced off.

The headline quite simply read: 'The New Beetle Cabriolet.'

Look up minimalist ads today and you'll find more of this ilk. The industry refers to them as 'clever-clever', as they favour visual double meanings. They work by manipulating or reducing a familiar visual. Due to the fact that the average person sees 3,000 to 20,000 messages a day, our visual recognition skills are acute, enabling us to detect the most subtle of these subversions and share the in-joke. We're flattered by understanding visual trickery, despite missing it at first glance.

To finish on a return to fast food, take McDonald's advert for their in-store Wi-Fi (also from DDB, 2009). First the viewer sees the Wi-Fi symbol, and at a second glance they see it's been constructed by three carefully placed fries of differing sizes. In this simple realization, the ad has communicated and been remembered.

Advertising, more than any other visual medium, begs, borrows and steals. It evolves by optimizing its message. And, of course, it builds on its previous successes. These elements can be boiled down in part and applied to the new. They can become tricks of recognition or tone-setters for truthful stories. Sometimes these methods can be insisted upon as a rule, or taken for shorthand, or a shortcut. Once they're rendered and revered, they're usually set for a while. But either way they become fodder for adaptation and counter-use. White Space ideals have dominated print advertising since Volkswagen in the 1950s. It is used to deliver product truth. But the thing that made 'Think Small' and 'Lemon' so endearing was their context – their point of difference. Minimum was the antidote to a culture of maximum.

Similarly, Beetle ownership allowed you to show off that you didn't need to show off. Those who appreciate minimalism define things by deciding what to leave out.

Simon Kirkham is a creative director/copywriter who has worked in many ad agencies, including Leo Burnett, Ogilvy & Mather and Tribal DDB.

SIMPLIFICATION TODAY

We live in an environment of constant communication, bombarded by switched-on imagery. But not everyone signs up for this, and a growing number of people are opting out of the digital revolution and choosing to live a simple way of life.

By Stuart Tolley

'Any intelligent fool can make things bigger, more complex…
It takes a touch of genius, and a lot of courage, to move in the
opposite direction.' E.F. Schumacher

For most of us, modern life is full of plenty. At times, too much so. How much of a good thing really is enough? How much of anything, regardless of its quality, is too much? Possessions, food, information – even money brings responsibilities and choices that can become burdensome. And what is a good life? In an increasingly connected and 'switched on' world, we are faced more than ever with the reality of the widening gulf between those who have and those who have not, and with the reality of finite resources as our planet becomes depleted. It's no surprise that there is a growing movement of people who, when faced with this burden and dose of reality, choose to make significant changes to their lives, adopting and promoting 'simple living' in some way, shape or form.

Simple living is nothing new. It's a healthy tradition that dates back 3,000 years and has emerged independently as a philosophy of life in almost every civilization. The idea is to resist material desires with a resultant benefit in other areas of life, such as more time and energy for creativity, to enjoy and support friends and family, to provide services in the community, or to reduce one's impact upon the earth and its resources. Simple living can include many different practices but usually includes reducing one's possessions, slowing down, stripping away clutter and creating more space (whether physically or psychologically). It's not difficult to see why the lifestyle is often referred to as

'minimalist'. Essentially, the two ideals have much in common. They are both purposeful and intentional. Indeed, simple living is distinct from those forced to live frugally or in poverty through no choice of their own. But minimalism goes beyond simplicity – it's a conscious design or style where the simplest and fewest elements are used, crucially, to create the maximum effect. As we have seen throughout this book, minimalism does not always mean austerity. Nor does it mean an absence of luxury, with many adopters investing in high-quality, expensive items but ones that are durable and timeless. What you call it isn't as important as how you live it – whether simple living or minimalism, how are these ideals manifesting themselves in people's lives today? And does this impact upon design?

Creating a 'capsule wardrobe' appears to be a key tenet for many people seeking to adopt and promote a 'simple' lifestyle. Curating a smaller collection of clothes and accessories and choosing coordinating clothes of higher, more durable quality which can be mixed and matched means fewer possessions. This can be a backlash against cheap, throwaway fashion and its impact upon both the environment and the people at the lowest end of the fashion chain, but for many a reduced wardrobe also means less time, effort and energy wasted on making decisions about non-essential things. President Barack Obama explains his own limited fashion choices as follows: 'I wear only gray or blue suits. I'm trying to pare down decisions. I don't want to make decisions about what I'm eating or wearing. Because I have too many other decisions to make.'

A simple wardrobe seldom means a slouchy, lazy look. It's about feeling 'put together', even creating a personal uniform, a brand. Alice Gregory, a writer living in Brooklyn, thinks 'wearing the same outfit every day is a way of asserting your status as a protagonist' in life. Well-recognized proponents of a personal uniform are Steve Jobs, who wore black turtlenecks and jeans, and Mark Zuckerberg, with his grey t-shirt and hoodie. Their choice of uniform implies 'functionality', but, ultimately, this has become fashionable, with the emergence of Normcore in 2014 – the wearing of clothes so anonymous and democratic that the wearers could be 'art kids or middle-aged, middle-American tourists'. A basic style flies in the face of high fashion, and one can even see it as an avoidance of any obvious display of wealth in a world where poverty persists.

But true minimalist fashion moves beyond basic and doesn't mean anonymous. Minimalism creates shapes that are striking, with clean lines, angularity and crisp tailoring. Think of Coco Chanel in the 1920s, daring to simplify garments to make them more comfortable and functional for women after the pre-First World War bows, pleats and bustles and the beads and fringes of the Jazz Age. As maximalist and minimalist fashions have continued to cycle through the eras, *Vogue* fashion director Kate Phelan sees the surge of fashion bloggers who 'wear a mish-mashed "look at me" style' forcing a pared-down response, 'a restraint in the industry'.

Some designers, such as Gareth Pugh and Hussein Chalayan, continue to embrace minimalism in all its geometric, monochromatic glory, reminiscent of the fashion movement's apogee in the 1960s, creating futuristic sculptures that couldn't be further from wardrobe basics. But such brands as Céline and Jil Sander (who collaborated successfully with Japanese retailer Uniqlo to create a slew of wardrobe 'staples') aim to strike a balance with clothing that is simple and clutter-free but creative. And Nordic labels such as Acne, Sand, Tiger of Sweden and Filippa K offer smart, pared-down pieces. Anne Christine Persson, vice president and development director of Copenhagen Fashion Week, remarks, 'Our brands have an appealing image. If you compare Nordic design to French fashion, it's typically very high fashion and complicated, while UK fashion is more street and quirky, Italian design tends to be a bit over the top and US fashion has a sporty edge. Nordic fashion manages to encompass it all, without being too much of anything – making our brands very understated and clean-cut.'

Living a simple life and advocating minimalism are conscious choices, but the times of austerity in much of the Western world since the economic crises of 2008 onwards have imposed their own limitations. Consider the difficulties faced by a generation of young adults who would have been eager nest-fleers, but are now either staying at or returning home to live with their parents or other family members due to a lack of employment opportunities and the scarcity of affordable homes to buy or, in some major cities, even to rent.

'A basic style flies in the face of high fashion, and one can even see it as an avoidance of any obvious display of wealth in a world where poverty persists.'

In Spain nearly half of young adults (18–29-year-olds) live with their parents, precipitating a modern design challenge of accommodating an adult in a space previously occupied by a child or adolescent. Spain's PKMN Architecture firm created the concept of 'Home Back Home', reinventing the 'kid's' room with modular, flexible, low-cost furniture components and pared-back decoration.

Co-living and co-working are becoming ever more prevalent in times when people are unwilling or unable to take a large financial risk to set up a home or business. In major urban centres, this gap in the market is being met by a raft of shared workspace developments, even work/living spaces. Catering to a young, professional audience who can't afford large properties, who aren't starting families just yet and who are more interested in work and leisure than accumulating 'stuff', these spaces are often an exercise in pared-down, minimalist living. In London, The Collective, a property development and management company, has created four buildings based on the 'micro-housing' ethos. The Collective's founder Reza Merchant states, 'An increasing shortage of space, coupled with an increasing population means we are forced to come up with solutions to the

housing crisis. Micro-housing is not exploitative if well designed. With the right, innovative design, use of space can be maximized efficiently – it's little things, like clever shelves to partition the kitchenette from the bed that can also be used as storage space and are also a cool piece of furniture.'

It is not all about modern, urban living, however. The burgeoning 'Tiny House' movement sees downsizers from all walks of life choosing to design and build their own homes under 400 square feet (in comparison, the typical American home is around 2,600 square feet and British homes are around 818 square feet). This has thrown up a plethora of designs, not least because people are building their homes from scratch around their own lifestyle. This is the freedom enjoyed by people becoming their own architects and interior designers – in reality, the results aren't always pretty but with the liberating quality of constraint, the response always favours functionality over superfluity.

And it's not only about frugal times. With wealth comes the freedom of choice and, for many, this means choosing a truly minimalist design at home – one that doesn't necessarily come cheap. It can cost a fortune to make things look simple. When you consider a minimalist home that showcases plain

'In true minimalist style, this results not only in reduction but a new ability to use the "things" in your life to maximum effect – to inspire happiness.'

walls without decorative papers, with large expanses of floor uncovered by carpets or rugs, and large furniture items uncluttered by soft furnishings, then materials and finishes matter. You need top-quality materials and workmanship for smooth walls, polished floors and furniture that can speak for itself. John Pawson, a British architectural designer talks about a retrospective of his work, *Plain Space*, at the Design Museum in London in 2010. 'It's very easy to misunderstand the work. People…think it's all about nothing. They think it's easy to produce these rooms and places.' Rowan Moore reflected on Pawson's work, describing how he was 'removing superfluity from interiors so that you could better appreciate their qualities of light, proportion and material. [But] amid the restraint and austerity there would be the luxury of stuff, such as the veins of marble or the grain of wood.'

Smaller living spaces, or even the large, minimalist homes with expensive finishes described above, demand less clutter. This ensures that the well-designed interior retains its ability to bring calm and focus, perhaps room to breathe, think and create. It also allows those possessions purposefully chosen for display to be better appreciated – the design allows objects to come to the fore.

There is a surging industry in blogs, books, lifestyle courses and bespoke services aiming to help us become 'free' of possessions, to 'de-clutter' our lives and to embrace simple living. Consider the trajectory of Marie Kondo, a Japanese 'tidying-up consultant', whose book *The Life-Changing Magic of Tidying Up* topped the *New York Times* bestseller list. In 2015 she was selected as one of the 100 most influential people in the world by *Time* magazine. She advocates a method of organization known as the KonMari method, which consists of gathering together everything you own and then keeping only those things that 'spark joy'. In true minimalist style, this results not only in reduction but a new ability to use the 'things' in your life to maximum effect – to inspire happiness. Joshua Fields Millburn and Ryan Nicodemus, writing as 'The Minimalists' both online and in books, are similarly keen to acknowledge that minimalism is not about getting rid of clutter but about a deeper exploration of our relationship with 'things'. What meaning do we give to material possessions? What is truly important in life?

The breakneck pace of innovation and design allows us to jettison things that have only existed previously as physical objects and to turn increasingly to digital formats, which take

GEO
METRY

ERASED
TAPES
RECORDS

Interview Matthew Lee
Photograph Ivan Jones

Erased Tapes Records was founded in London in 2007 by German-born Robert Raths and is home to musicians such as Nils Frahm, Ólafur Arnalds, Kiasmos and Michael Price. Supermundane, also known as Rob Lowe, is an artist, graphic designer and illustrator who created the cover art for *Odyssey*, a 2013 album by Erased Tapes artist Rival Consoles. Torsten Posselt is one third of Berlin digital crafts studio FELD, and a regular Erased Tapes collaborator.

Would you say Erased Tapes is a minimalist record label?

ROBERT: Absolutely. Obviously the label is minimalist graphically but also we barely have any groups on the label; it's mostly solo artists. Music pioneer Lubomyr Melnyk is described as a maximalist because he plays a lot of notes on the piano, but to me he's an absolute minimalist. He's focused on one instrument his whole life. We're living in an age where so much is noisy and flashy. There's a certain beauty in having just one colour.

How important is packaging to Erased Tapes?

ROBERT: Packaging is not so much a product as an opportunity to create an introduction to the artist's mind, to the music's soul. It's like the first chapter in a book or the beginning of a film. It puts people into a certain environment before the music even begins; it prepares you for the journey. The early covers were made myself, with the exception of Ólafur Arnalds' artwork. I would spend hours on night buses listening to the music, envisaging what would be the best way to present it in visual form. I always had a 'less is more' approach. I wanted to keep the artwork universally accessible but also create something iconic that grabs you.

Was it a risk starting a record label, especially one with a focus on packaging, in 2007, when sales of records were in free-fall?

ROBERT: It certainly was. It was around the time Radiohead gave their music away [*In Rainbows* was released digitally on a pay-what-you-want basis] and I care a lot about the tangible aspect of packaging, and combining that analogue history with digital intelligence. That had an uncertain future. I hadn't been part of the music industry at all. I didn't know what I was about to do. I went to the bank simply to open an account and the account manager advised me that it wasn't a good idea to start a record label in 2007.

Were you a musician at the time?

ROBERT: I was, although I had studied architecture. That's why I came to London in the first place. Music took me away from architecture, but I still think of what I do as some type of architecture in the way I approach it.

How did your logo evolve?

ROBERT: I was trying to create a logo in line with the name, something with erasing and tapes, and it felt so forced and literal. That's not what I wanted. Instead, I wanted something almost invisible, more like an atmosphere. The mountain became the logo because I was fascinated by this guy I found on Myspace, who made these paintings on these seismographic discs you use to measure earthquakes. I like the dialogue, the mathematics of it. When you look closely it's got 24 hours on it, like day and night. To me that's music – depth and time.

Why do you use the name Supermundane, Rob?
SUPERMUNDANE: There's a very famous Hollywood actor called Rob Lowe and I couldn't get roblowe.com.

What's your background?
SUPERMUNDANE: I was working at Ministry of Sound, doing covers for trance albums and things like art-directing bikini-clad girls in Ibiza. Somehow my work got picked up on the American West Coast skateboard scene in the late 1990s and after that I worked at magazines like *Sleazenation* and *Anorak*. At the moment I purely do my personal work and some commissions such as a mural for Dolby Sound in Los Angeles.

How did your collaboration with Erased Tapes for the Rival Consoles artwork happen?
SUPERMUNDANE: Ryan Lee West [Rival Consoles] is a neighbour of mine. My style had been getting more minimalist and graphic, so we thought we'd try collaborating. I was sent the music for *Odyssey*, or at least early versions of the songs, which isn't always the case when you do record covers. Ryan had quite a few opinions on the visual direction, and so I went through lots of iterations before this final version came about.

Your earlier work was mostly hand-drawn, intricate line-work. But you've since shifted to a bolder, more geometric style…
SUPERMUNDANE: I made that shift around 2010. Before then I was using these simple black lines and creating optical effects without perspective, trying to create depth and movement, which I still do now but in a different way. I got fed up of people calling them doodles, even though they were very constructed and carefully drawn. I began to zoom into the detail, see how small areas are constructed and enlarge them. That kind of legitimizes the process. I looked at how the lines interacted and how they sit on top of each other to create depth; it's almost like they're under a microscope. It's like taking one spot from my older work and then reducing it as far as possible. It has the same movement and depth and optical effects, but in a more minimalist way. I've reduced the artwork further still, down to 45-degree lines and two colours, which are then repeated to create new compositions.

Your Erased Tapes work only uses black and white colours…
SUPERMUNDANE: For the Michael Price and Rival Consoles covers it's purely black-and-white line-work, which developed from my personal work. It was just playing around with connected lines, depth and optical effects.

What's your background, Torsten?
TORSTEN: I studied civil engineering because I wanted to do something to pay the bills, but after a while I craved something more artistic. I worked at a printing company to learn how books are made and I later went to Berlin's

University of the Arts, which is where I met Benjamin Maus and Frederic Gmeiner. We co-founded FELD four years ago and we have focused on digital art – building our own tools, lots of programming and physical computing. I maintained a passion for graphic design and designed lots of techno flyers and posters, which were super-heavy and colourful with lots of textures. It seems like madness compared to what I do now.

Why did you move towards a more minimalist style?
TORSTEN: I feel comfortable with minimalism and it calms me down. Everything seems to move so fast these days and our studio work is also fast-paced and based around technology. Minimalist artwork is a bit like medicine for me. Some people do drugs – I do minimalist artwork.

How did your relationship with Erased Tapes begin?
TORSTEN: Through Nils Frahm. We were flatmates for six or seven years and we're always on the same page, so my relationship with Erased Tapes started as soon as Nils signed to them.

How did the collaboration for the Michael Price cover art happen?
SUPERMUNDANE: I'd already done the art for a project called *Connected Lines Studies*, a 20-page black-and-white booklet. I was experimenting with line-work and depth in this booklet; you can use a minimal amount of greys and still create lots of depth.
TORSTEN: Robert and I felt that the optical effects of Rob's work were a perfect match for Michael Price's music and ideas. Rob handed over his complete selection and I picked the two

illustrations I felt were most striking. It became quite clear that Rob's illustrations should serve as the key visual for the cover artwork so I just had to create a design around his work.

As the label boss, how much are you involved in creating cover art, Robert?
ROBERT: It depends on the artist and the project. For *Odyssey*, I was the distant voice that looks at it more neutrally because Rob and Ryan are neighbours and they were hanging out and working on it. Sometimes the musicians aren't that involved and then it's more between me and whoever does the cover. I like it best when the three heads – the musician, the artist and the label curator – come together.

What's the concept for the geometric cover art on the Kiasmos EP?
ROBERT: Kiasmos was a new project by Ólafur Arnalds and Janus Rasmussen, and they didn't have a visual identity at the start. Part of the job of designing the first 12-inch cover was creating a logo that would become their identity. So that's what we commissioned Torsten to do.
TORSTEN: I did it with a friend, Kay Damme. We were basically jamming, to be honest, smoking and drinking beer and drawing – not on paper, but straight onto the screen. It was obvious it had to be iconic and our first idea involved a pyramid for the visual direction. We wanted to make it look three-dimensional without it actually being three-dimensional. For the second EP and album we were able to adjust and manipulate this pyramid design.

'Everything seems to move so fast these days and our studio work is also fast-paced and based around technology. Minimalist artwork is a bit like medicine for me. Some people do drugs – I do minimalist artwork.'

There's no type on the Kiasmos cover. Why's that?
TORSTEN: I'm a huge typographic nerd and I love micro-typography. If it were up to me I'd make my typography as small as possible. But I'm not a fan of having a word mark and a logo in combination. I prefer everything to work by itself.

On the cover of Seven Fingers by Nils Frahm and Anne Müller the type is tiny...
TORSTEN: Nils hates me for doing this! Actually at the beginning he loved me and now he's saying he wants the type a bit bigger. He says it's now too small to read.

Speaking of small, how does working with CDs compare to working with vinyl?
ROBERT: We still make an effort with CDs – we have them in cardboard packaging and they're mostly printed inside-out. I always hated jewel cases and digipacks with plastic trays, and I wanted to bring back the feel of real paper, something that can age and stain. A gatefold in a CD can remind you of vinyl and hopefully point you in the direction of vinyl records.
TORSTEN: I think we all can agree that vinyl is the thing. Size matters. Vinyl gives you freedom and space.
SUPERMUNDANE: I grew up with vinyl, so for me holding the sleeve in my hands is part of the process of enjoying the music.

CDs were in crappy plastic cases and then it went down to little jpegs. So the return of vinyl is wonderful. People are paying more attention to production now.

How do you find the right balance between spending money on quality packaging and selling vinyl at the right price?
ROBERT: One of the things I love about working with Torsten is that he always pushes me out of the comfort zone that's determined by finances. In the beginning I was the bad guy saying that, while I know it would be amazing, I'd have people complaining that it's too expensive. But sometimes you simply can't compromise, like with the Erased Tapes fifth-anniversary box set. The time we all invested in that box set makes it priceless. It's an artefact, you know.
TORSTEN: I think that's really important, to create an artefact, something that hopefully lasts a long time. Sometimes I become obsessed with making something better and higher quality. And sometimes you can lose yourself on this path of trying to make something better. I need to be restrained sometimes.
ROBERT: So much is overproduced nowadays. It's easy to throw every bell and whistle at something. It takes confidence to strip it down. That's an important part of minimalism – restraint.

Robert Raths, Torsten Posselt and Rob Lowe (Supermundane) were photographed at Elephant and Castle, London

SUPERMUNDANE/FELD
ERASED TAPES RECORDS

Erased Tapes Records is a London-based independent record label focusing on the release of minimal/avant-garde music with a roster of contemporary classical composers including Nils Frahm, Ólafur Arnalds and Michael Price.

Stylistically, the direction of cover artwork has been refined by label founder Robert Raths since the label's inception in 2007, and recent releases focus on a clean, crisp, geometric approach, which is often accompanied by a muted colour palette. The artwork is created by a small roster of contributing artists including Berlin-based Torsten Posselt and London-based Rob Lowe, aka Supermundane, and beautifully reflects the label's contemporary interpretation of classical avant-garde and ambient music.

Publisher Erased Tapes Records
Art Direction Robert Raths
Design Torsten Posselt (FELD), Rob Lowe (Supermundane)
Origin UK, Germany

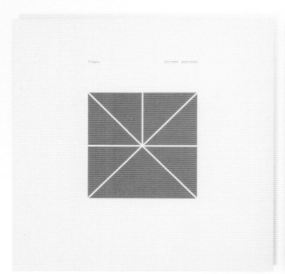

TOKO DESIGN
PTW ARCHITECTS

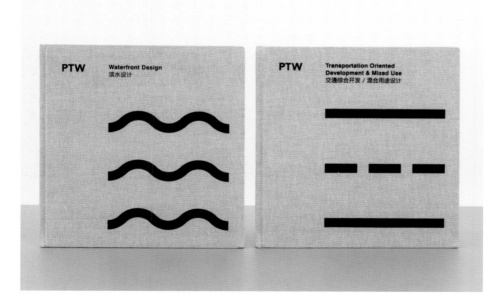

PTW Architects (formerly Peddle Thorp & Walker) were established in Sydney by James Peddle in 1889. Samuel George Thorp was made a partner soon after his award-winning entry for Sydney's first planned garden suburb, Daceyville, in 1912. With a rich Australian history, the firm have been responsible for most of the harbour waterfront development opportunities in Sydney, most recently with Rogers Stirk Harbour on the Barangaroo project.

To celebrate their 125th anniversary, PTW turned to Sydney-based studio Toko, renowned for creating classic design, to develop a series of nine Japanese-English books to reflect key areas of the firm's expertise and history.

Toko designed a temporary identity for the project and a series of nine bold graphic emblems as a central feature on the cloth-bound covers. Each emblem reduces the individual specialism to an instantly recognizable and confident icon, ranging from *Sports & Olympic*, *Culture & the Arts*, *Waterfront Design*, *Transportation Oriented Development and Mixed Use*, *Health and Aged Care* and *Urban Planning and Design*.

Publisher PTW Architects
Art Direction & Design Toko Design
Production Shanghai Shentian Printing Co.
Origin Australia

DESIGNBOLAGET
WON HUNDRED

Danish fashion brand Won Hundred state that they have an 'appreciation for simplicity and understated design'. The brand champion a minimalist aesthetic: 'We want the personality of the user to transcend through Won Hundred's designs. This way every piece becomes unique.'

To capture this ethos across all their visual communications, Won Hundred commissioned Copenhagen-based design studio Designbolaget. As creative director Claus Due says, 'We'd worked with the brand for a while but in 2013 they approached us with a wish to strengthen their identity, make it more coherent, something that was reflected in their new collections with clean, simple shapes. So, we developed an identity founded on one simple graphic shape, the frame with the triangles inside of it.'

Due explains that the geometric shape is actually derived from Irving Penn's studio set-up. The American photographer worked extensively in fashion. 'He's one of our photographic heroes. He shot portraits in a narrow built corner. We borrowed this idea and created a graphic shape out of a corner, which we then used in both the art direction and as a graphic element.'

The simple approach provided longevity and transferability. As Due notes, 'It translated well across a variety of different formats, including printed matter, t-shirts, paper bags and hang tags.'

Art Direction & Graphic Design Claus Due (Designbolaget)
Origin Denmark

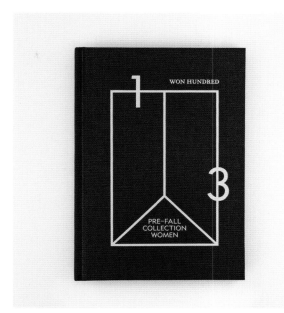

BUILD
STUDIO AVES

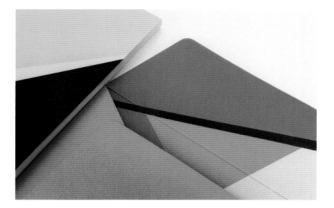

Studio Aves, a UK design practice launched in 2014, specialize in typefaces and typographic design. Design studio Build were commissioned to create an ingenious identity for Studio Aves (*aves* means bird in Latin). As Michael C. Place explains, 'We designed a colour-based identity for this typographic design studio around the markings of British birds. These include a great spotted woodpecker, a blue tit, a goldfinch, a magpie, a dunnock, a wood warbler, a wheatear, a kingfisher and a robin.'

To cut costs on a relatively low print run, items such as the business cards, compliments card and DL envelope were digitally printed on different-coloured Colorplan stock. This resulted in the look and feel of a hi-spec print at a lower production cost. This simple, geometric identity runs across a variety of printed material, including business cards, a letterhead and stickers.

The result is aesthetically beautiful, drawing distinctive value from a good contrast of colour and basic geometric forms based on a simple but abstract ornithological concept linking it to the studio's name. The mechanical qualities of mono-spaced slab and sans-serif characters offer a stripped-down functionality alongside the edge-to-edge flourish and striking excess of colour. This contrast is mirrored in the print's balance of economy and the perception of high quality it achieves.

Art Direction & Design Michael C. Place (Build)
Production Generation Press
Origin UK

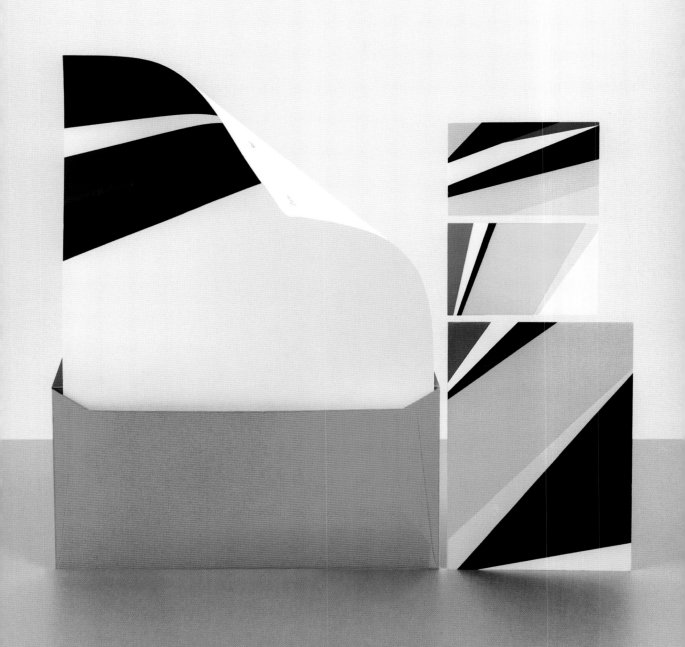

MAGPIE STUDIO
RANDOM DANCE: MIND AND MOVEMENT

Wayne McGregor, a UK choreographer, established the Mind and Movement project to revolutionize the way dance is taught. He commissioned Magpie Studio, a London-based graphic design agency, who devised a typographic solution that allowed the key principles of McGregor's methods to be illustrated without suggestive photographs of dancers.

The *Choreographic Thinking Tools* included printed and digital resources for dance tutors, which were supported by an interactive exhibition in London at the Wellcome Trust, a charitable foundation dedicated to improving health.

Art Direction David Azurdia, Ben Christie (Magpie Studio)
Design Ben Christie, Aimi Awang, Jack Beverage (Magpie Studio)
Origin UK

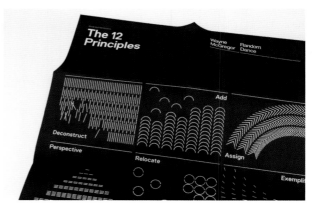

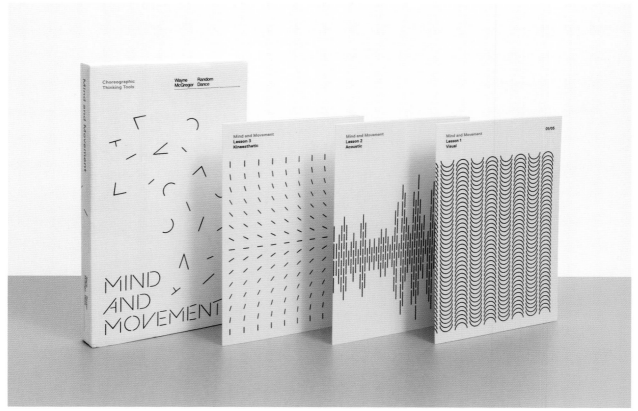

ENA CARDENAL DE LA NUEZ
THE JAPANESE GARDEN

The Japanese Garden was an exhibition that confronted the work of the Japanese landscape architect Mirei Shigemori through a series of works created in collaboration with artists such as Richard Serra, Cildo Meireles, Yoko Ono and Antoni Tàpies. It established a cultural and artistic dialogue between East and West by looking at elements that are common to both and transcend possible cultural, spatial and temporal limits.

A Spanish- and English-language catalogue, published by the Madrid cultural centre, La Casa Encendida, to accompany the exhibition, was art-directed by Ena Cardenal de la Nuez, a Spanish graphic designer renowned for her simplified and often geometric approach to book design. A typographic cover was created to illustrate the group exhibition, with the title in Spanish, English and Japanese. The title is divided into vertical and horizontal planes occupying the spaces, like a projected garden.

Publisher La Casa Encendida, Alicia Chillida, Patronato de la Alhambra y Generalife
Art Direction & Design Ena Cardenal de la Nuez
Production Antonio Rubio, TF Artes Gráficas
Origin Spain

KAROSHI
MYELOMA UK

Myeloma UK is a charitable organization that provides support for those suffering from a rare form of cancer of the bone marrow. To help raise funds and awareness, a regular music event called Reachin' was launched, held at the Turner Contemporary Gallery in Margate. The identity for the event was created by London-based graphic design consultancy Karoshi who drew inspiration from the architecture of the venue – specifically, the distinctive mono-pitched roof structure and gallery

windows by David Chipperfield Architects.

'The event is about music', explains Ben Vincent, creative partner at Karoshi. 'It was important for us to have a visual reference to that through the brand-mark. There is a double-height window in the gallery which features a circular motif and the way that the panes were separated reminded us of a speaker grill. Distilling this down to the simplest form allowed us to integrate it into the grid and graphic patterns.'

A grid was constructed from a series of equilateral triangles and was expanded over a series of events with a different colour palette assigned to each. The only constants were the charity's orange and the white brand-mark.

The resulting artwork was a beautifully realized response to the brief to engage a younger demographic while raising funds.

Art Direction Ben Vincent,
Gavin Ireland (Karoshi)
Design Jacqui Browne
Production Impress
Origin UK

TWOPOINTS.NET
MAPPING JABAL AL NATHEEF

Mapping Jabal Al Natheef analyses one of most populous informal refugee settlements in east Amman, Jordan. It is the result of a ten-day extensive mapping workshop hosted by Arini, a non-profit private study and research institution that seeks out aspiring designers from around Jordan and brings them together with local and international academics and professionals.

For TwoPoints.Net, this was an important design project. 'The book is about a degraded area in Amman, one of the most problematic Palestinian refugee camps in Jordan. Yet, we felt strongly that the book does not have to express "material poverty". It is about people, there is a huge, human energy that we wanted to highlight... The thickness of the cover was especially controlled. We wanted the book to have the appearance of a notebook because it was the result of a workshop, where participants were taking notes and making hand drawings. That's why it was also important that it was flexible. We chose a rough, ivory paper, with a lot of texture, called volume paper – it has the advantage of being thick but very light, so it makes the book thicker but not heavier.'

The geometric lines on the cover are Arini's visual identity, also developed by TwoPoints.Net. The cover itself is white cloth, printed with turquoise and metallic copper stamping. The book is printed in just two colours, though this rule is broken in one important way, 'There were some full colour pictures of the landscape and we did not want to convert these into monochrome, so we placed them at the beginning and at the end of the book, like endpapers.'

Publisher Arini
Design TwoPoints.Net
Production Agpograf
Origin Jordan

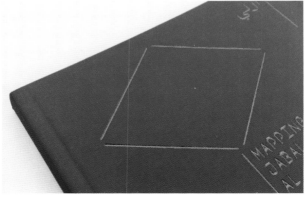

MANUAL
GOOGLE MATERIAL PRINTED KIT

Manual are a San Francisco-based visual communication studio founded by Tom Crabtree. The studio were invited by Google to create a visual language for the Material Printed Kit presented at their launch at the 2014 I/O Conference. It was a guide for the Google Material Design interface based on 'the classic principles of good design combined with the innovation and possibility of technology and science'.

The geometric design was taken directly from Google's interface design, as Crabtree explains: 'We took the basic form of the rectangle and used it in different ways to express concepts within the design language such as depth, movement, action and animation.' The purpose of the printed kit was to express the core design foundation behind Material Design. 'We deliberately avoided relying on any images of the user interface in the design, and instead used foundational elements of graphic design (colour, form, composition) to express

the content. This led to a more conceptual artefact.' Given the minimalist nature of the design, it was essential that the physicality of the kit enhanced the design. It was printed in ten spot colours with uncoated and high-gloss card stocks, blind embossing, debossing, die-cuts, spot varnishes and hand-applied card elements.

Publisher Google
Art Direction Tom Crabtree (Manual)
Design Tom Crabtree, Tanner Irwin, Eileen Lee, Caroline Reece, Jerod Rivera
Production Oscar Printing
Origin USA

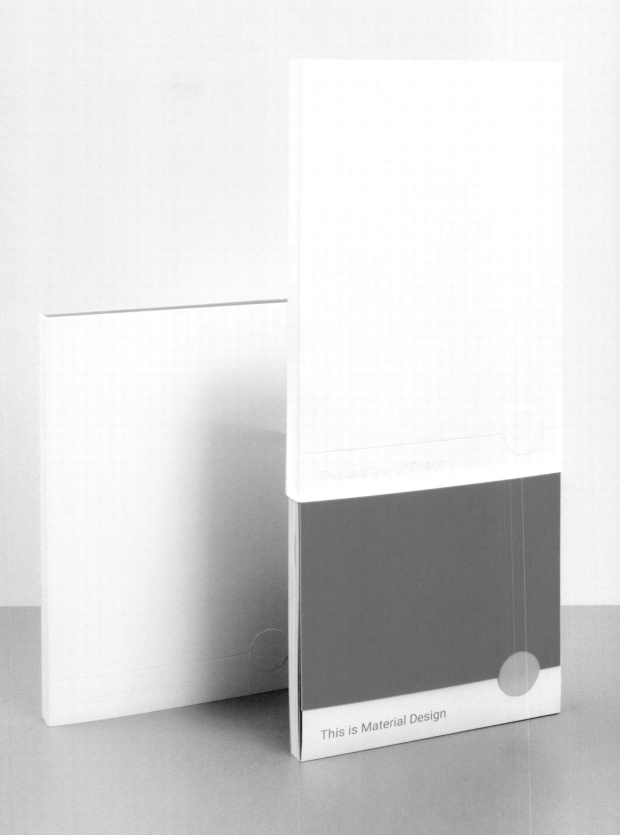

This is Material Design

PATRICK FRY
SHAKESPEARE'S GLOBE

Shakespeare's Globe hosts Interface, an annual digital networking event that enables digital artists, designers and developers to meet some of the UK's top culture brands. In 2014, the organizers sought out Patrick Fry. He built a new identity around four circular motifs, separated into ten pieces to represent the number of partners at the event. For Fry, 'Shakespeare's Globe, both by name and by its architecture, has always been associated with the simple circle. It was important that the circles connected...as a reference to networking.'

Publisher Shakespeare's Globe: Interface
Art Direction & Design Patrick Fry
Origin UK

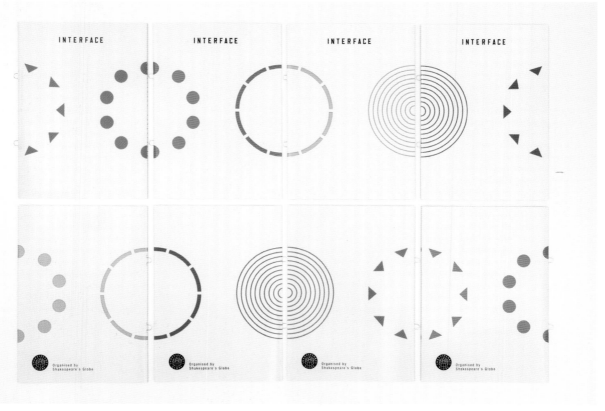

TWICE
VILLA NOAILLES

Twice are an art-direction studio based in Paris. The studio create work for clients in the music, fashion and arts industries, including Villa Noailles in Hyères. An early example of French modernist architecture, the villa was built in 1923 by architect Robert Mallet-Stevens for art patrons Charles and Marie-Laure de Noailles. It is now a cultural arts centre.

The Villa Noailles foundation curates numerous contemporary design and architecture events, including a support platform called Design Parade, which encourages young artists to meet and discuss design with professional practitioners.

Each year editorial documents are published to highlight the programming, adorned by a minimalist, abstract cover design created by Twice. As art directors Fanny and Clémentine explain, 'Our design represents the works of all the designers shown during the festival, rather than a single image. Abstraction is important as it sets the tone without saying too much while keeping a coherence throughout the global communication of the festival.'

Publisher Archibooks, Villa Noailles
Art Direction Villa Noailles, Fanny Le Bras, Clémentine Berry (Twice)
Production Imprimerie CCI
Origin France

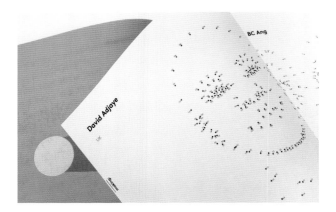

GARBETT
MAKING CONFERENCE

Making Conference, organized by the Australian Institute of Architects, is an exploration of the role of the architect as a maker of environments. The 2014 event had four sections (making culture, making life, making connections and making impact) which became the inspiration for the geometric design created by Sydney-based graphic design studio Garbett.

The primary audience for the event is architects, so it was important to create a rational design. A colour was assigned to each of the four sections and an alphabetic dot matrix was developed from the position of each letter name, 'making' it appear as it does in the alphabet when placed in a grid of four letters wide. This design was sometimes overlapped to create an almost random composition, which resonates with the festival's making theme.

The dot-matrix theme was enhanced throughout the supporting printed material. Different-coloured perspex lanyards, which were laser-cut and engraved, were designed to be worn around the neck of attendees, to signal a pass for different levels of tickets. A join-the-dots illustration style was used for speaker portraits in the conference programme.

Publisher Australian Institute of Architects
Art Direction & Design Paul Garbett (Garbett)
Illustration Paul Garbett, Danielle de Andrade, Adam France
Production Spotpress, Green and Gold
Origin Australia

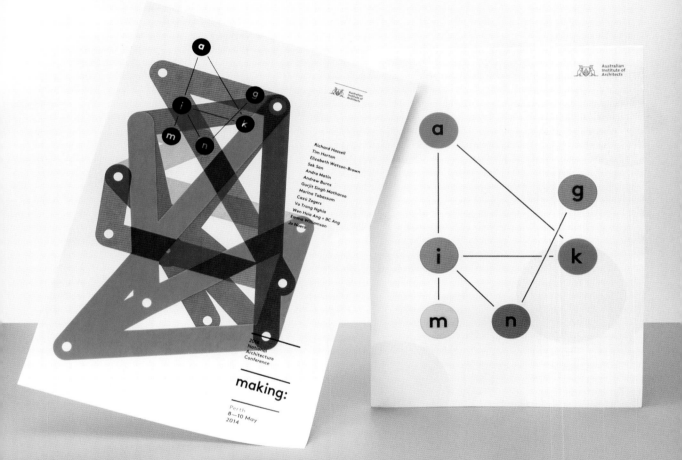

making:

2014 National Architecture Conference

Richard Hassell
Tim Horton
Elizabeth Watson-Brown
Sek San
Andra Matin
Andrew Burns
Gurjit Singh Matharoo
Marina Tabassum
Cazu Zegers
Vo Trong Nghia
Wen Hsia Ang + BC Ang
Emma Williamson
Jo Noero

Perth
8—10 May
2014

Australian Institute of Architects

NEUE
NORWEGIAN METEOROLOGICAL INSTITUTE

The mission of the Norwegian Meteorological Institute includes 'the protection of life and property'. It is important that visual communications are simple and clear – that weather forecasts and climatological reports are understandable to users, as well as impactful and trusted, and that the overall brand promotes its dependabilty and reliability. The creative team at Oslo-based design studio Neue understood this when they took on the brand strategy and visual identity, agreeing that 'whether you are a helicopter rescue pilot in the North Sea or just want to dress your children properly on a cold day, the Norwegian Meteorological Institute's identity must be recognizable and consistent.'

Lars Håvard Dahlstrøm and Benjamin Stenmarck reflect upon the key design elements: 'The circle and graph of the logo are an image of the knowledge the Norwegian Meteorological Institute needs to fulfil its task, climatological and meteorological research, as well as a free flow of data and information. It also offers associations to sun and sea, or moon and mountains.' Juxtaposed against the sober and clean design are a series of photos by world-renowned extreme-sports photographer Johan Wildhagen.

Publisher Norwegian Meteorological Institute
Art Direction Lars Håvard Dahlstrøm, Benjamin Stenmarck (Neue)
Design Lars Håvard Dahlstrøm, Benjamin Stenmarck, Nora Bremnæs
Photography Johan Wildhagen, Palookaville
Origin Norway

WANG ZHI–HONG
AND

Wang Zhi-Hong is a Taiwanese graphic designer who specializes in carefully considered, pared-back books and jackets, predominately for the book-publishing industry.

Commissioned by Garden City Publishing, *And* is a collection of works by the Taiwanese architectural photographer Lee Kuo-Min. The series of saddle-stitched books are housed in a grey box set adorned by a geometric cover design and bespoke typography.

The geometric cover design reflects Lee Kuo-Min's profession, as explained by Wang Zhi-Hong. 'An architectural photographer must identify the uniqueness in each subject, the existing building constructions, to convey the unique message within each given space. This awareness is reflected by the cubes and neutral triangles that make up the geometric typography on the cover, as they feature in numerous architectural subjects featured in the book.'

Publisher Garden City Publishing
Art Direction Wang Zhi-Hong
Photography Lee Kuo-Min
Production Chaw-Li Printing
Origin Taiwan

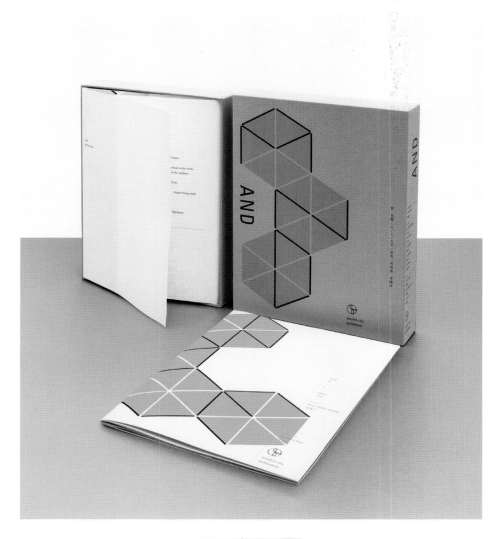

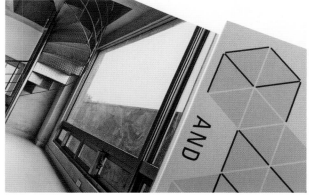

STOCKHOLM DESIGN LAB
NORDISKA MUSEET

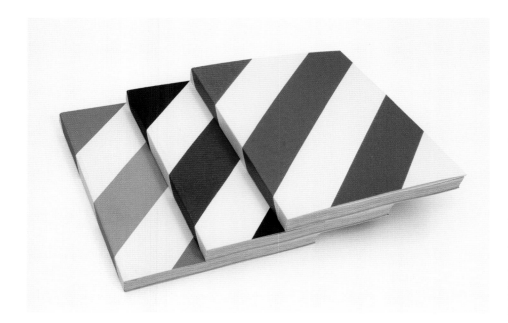

Nordiska Museet (The Nordic Museum) is a cathedral-like landmark situated on the Island of Djurgården in Stockholm. The museum, founded in the late 19th century, is Sweden's largest museum of cultural history.

For the exhibition *Stripes, Rhythm, Direction*, which opened in its grand hall in October 2013, the museum highlighted the role played by these aesthetics through 250 exhibits of art, architecture, design, crafts, science and landscape from the museum's collections.

Stockholm-based brand-design studio Stockholm Design Lab (SDL) was commissioned by the museum curator, Tom Hedqvist, to develop a unified identity for the exhibition: its promotion and signs, and a catalogue. The resulting design is an unashamedly contemporary and bold approach that features bright, broad diagonal bands of colour and a clear, modern, sans-serif typeface. Accompanying catalogues, adorned by different-coloured stripes, feature unique covers that were realized throughout the 1,500 printed copies. The final design direction was overwhelmingly positive and a radical visual departure for the museum, in contrast to the highly ornate architecture.

Art Direction Björn Kusoffsky (Stockholm Design Lab)
Design Lisa Fleck
Production Nordiska Museet
Origin Sweden

Ränder Rytm Riktning / Nordiska museet

4 oktober 2013 – 31 augusti 2014

NORDISKA MUSEET

The Jolt-Festival originated in Australia and reached Basel in 2014, presenting a broad spectrum of music. The Jolt LP from A Tree in a Field Records is a compilation that captures some of the best live performances from the festival. Shortly after its release, the Swiss ensemble Werktag approached the label, offering to release recordings of new pieces by Alex Buess, a member of the band Cortex featured on the Jolt LP, and Antoine Chessex. This allowed Swiss designer Marco Papiro to explore a visual analogy across the two releases as the label felt they would appeal to a similar audience.

A musician himself, Papiro is well versed in bringing design and music together; he is the creator of American musician Panda Bear's striking *Panda Bear Meets the Grim Reaper* LP. 'It all starts with the combination of letters I get to work with. Our alphabet is based on geometry, so the reduction to geometric forms seems quite obvious, though that is not what I'm primarily interested in, even if it might appear so at first glance! I let the rhythmic quality guide me. Once I've established a system, the result is largely self-generated, and often unpredictable. Playfulness and unpredictability are my main stimulations, and it reminds me a bit of a modular synthesizer, which is my other toy.'

Publisher A Tree in a Field Records
Art Direction & Design Marco Papiro
Production Handle With Care (Jolt), R.A.N.D. Muzik (Antoine Chessex/Werktag/Buess)
Origin Switzerland

JONATHAN BARNBROOK
A CLOCKWORK ORANGE

A Clockwork Orange by Anthony Burgess is a dystopian novel originally published by Penguin Books in 1962 and adapted as a film, directed by Stanley Kubrick, in 1971. On the 50th anniversary of the publication of the novel, Penguin art director Jim Stoddart commissioned graphic designer and typographer Jonathan Barnbrook to reimagine the paperback version of the cover. This special edition included restored text, interviews and reference material.

    Any rework of the original cover design was always going to be controversial and compared to David Pelham's famous original. Barnbrook's reimagining is intentionally bold and geometric, featuring only an orange circle that replaces part of the book title. As Barnbrook explains, 'After many years of doing what could be called "complex, layered design", I had reacted quite heavily against it by reducing my work down to the most basic essential elements.... On a very simple level it was to be as economic as possible, deleting a word from the title (a very brave thing for Penguin to do) and replacing it with a symbol of it – the orange circle to symbolize the word "orange". This was an acknowledgment of the stature of the book – it was so famous you could play with the title and people would still get it, but also it is a form of shorthand, how language is evolving for shorter attention spans.'

Publisher Penguin Books
Art Direction Jim Stoddart
Design Jonathan Barnbrook
Production Imogen Boase
Origin UK

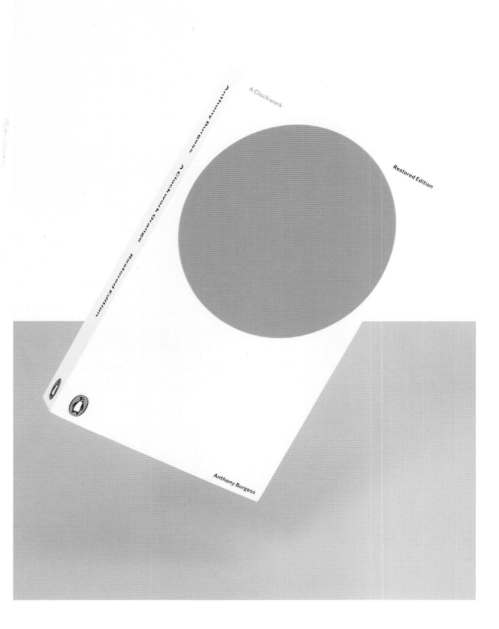

ALEX HUNTING & NATHALIE LEES
YOU CAN NOW

Established in 2001, You Can Now (YCN) is a global network that describes itself as 'an ever-growing family of creative thinkers and doers around the world'. Based in London, its members are primarily linked online and at events, but they also receive the print-based YCN magazine four times a year. Each issue takes on a theme, with writing commissioned from across the creative industries and enlivened by illustrators and photographers. Freed from having to compete on the news stand, the magazine can be bold in its approach. The creative force behind the magazine's visual identity, Alex Hunting, describes how 'we wanted to do something slightly different to what we were seeing around the independent magazine scene. This magazine has a refined and sophisticated aesthetic and is quite heavily influenced by 1960s publishing such as *Twen* and *Nova*.'

Publisher YCN Limited
Art Direction & Design Alex Hunting
Cover Illustration Nathalie Lees
Production Park Communications
Origin UK

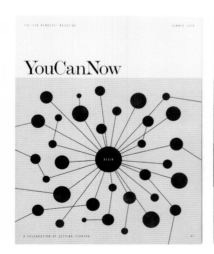
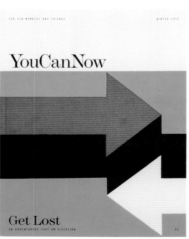
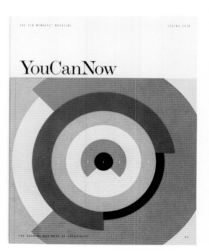

THE YCN MEMBERS' MAGAZINE

YouCanNow

WINTER 2014

Click
BECAUSE IT TAKES TWO TO TANGO

04

EDITED
HALF FULL, HALF EMPTY

Chet Lam's sixth book, *Half Empty, Half Full*, is a collection of 146 tips for city-dwellers to keep a clear head among the chaos of city life. Revolving around the idea of 'opposites', the paperback book explores this concept through five different categories.

To reflect the duality in the book's subject and the author's desired mental reflection of the reader, Hong Kong-based graphic design studio Edited used a cup of water as a visual metaphor. This design was enhanced by the embossed typography on the book jacket covered by a rough paper that, combined with the very pale green-and-white colour palette, creates the calm that is at odds with the noise and commotion of the city.

Publisher Kubrick
Art Direction & Design Renatus Wu (Edited)
Origin Hong Kong

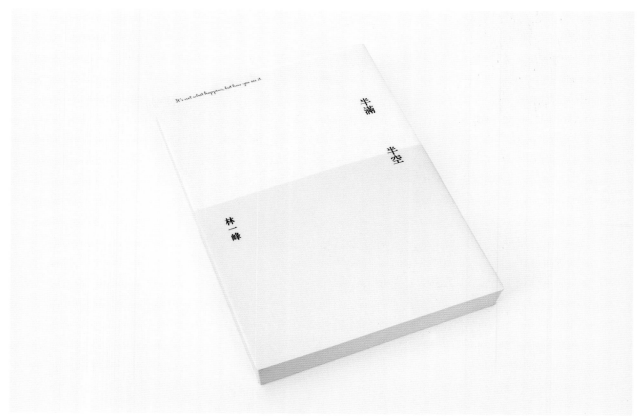

JONNY SANDERS
TELEMAN

Breakfast is the first album by London-based indie band Teleman. To reflect the minimal arrangement of instruments on the tracks and the clean, spacious production of the album, a geometric design was conceived.

This design was created by moving-image designer Jonny Sanders, who explains, 'the circles came from a video we made together for the single *Cristina*, which was very strict in its simplicity. It was immediately apparent that this should go on to form an identity for the band as it sat so well with the sound.'

The primary colours used for the circles were a direct reference to the *Cristina* video and formed the basis for the album design, merchandise and screen-printed tour poster. The reduced colour palette and geometric circles, arranged in a triangular formation, mean the cover artwork is instantly recognizable in different-sized formats. As Sanders says, 'I wanted to include a few different options for *Breakfast* so I added a reversible insert and a bonus sheet with a different pattern to appear behind the holes...this was something for people to interact with while they listen to the music.'

Publisher Moshi Moshi Records
Art Direction & Design Jonny Sanders
Screen Printing The Private Press
Production PIAS
Origin UK

SAWDUST
SHANGHAI RANKING 500

The Shanghai Jiao Tong Top 500 Research Universities Encyclopedia, or *Shanghai Ranking 500*, is an extensive book that features interviews with the leaders of the world's best 500 research universities as defined by the Academic Ranking of World Universities (ARWU).

London-based graphic design studio Sawdust, renowned for their typographic experiments, were commissioned to realize research developer Alisdair Jones's ambitious vision for the book. The book cover, chapter-opener pages and design details such as page numbers feature a geometric approach inspired by modernist architecture and the architectural photography of Matthias Heiderich. As Rob Gonzalez, design partner at Sawdust, explains, 'We had been exploring light and shadow in our work, a keen interest of ours, and so wanted to explore the possibility of creating typographic numerals using architectural shapes and lighting.'

The geometric typography directly references photographs of featured university buildings, which were supplied by *Shanghai Ranking 500*. Gonzalez continues, 'It appeared to us that these institutions take as much pride in their appearance as they do in their work, which is a compliment – some of the buildings are breathtaking to look at.'

Publisher SJTU Press, Alisdair Jones
Art Direction Rob Gonzalez, Jonathan Quainton (Sawdust)
Production SJTU Press
Origin China

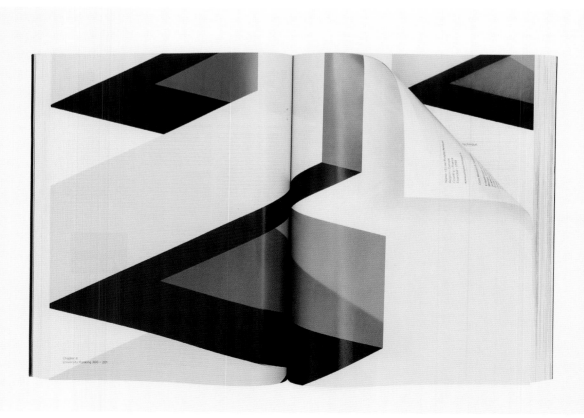

Shanghai Jiao Tong Top 500
Research Universities Encyclopedia
2014 – 2016

SHANGHAI
RANKING

HEY
NOTEBOOKS

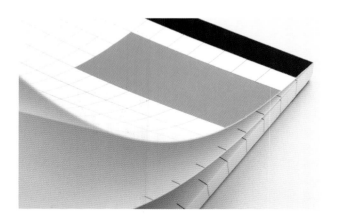

Hey are a graphic design studio based in Barcelona with a reputation for creating bright, reduced graphic solutions for lifestyle brands and art institutes. In 2013 Hey launched HeyShop, an online store selling self-initiated work, including the Hey gridded notebook. The simple geometric design reflects their overriding philosophy and design approach.

Art Direction Hey
Production Grafiko
Origin Spain

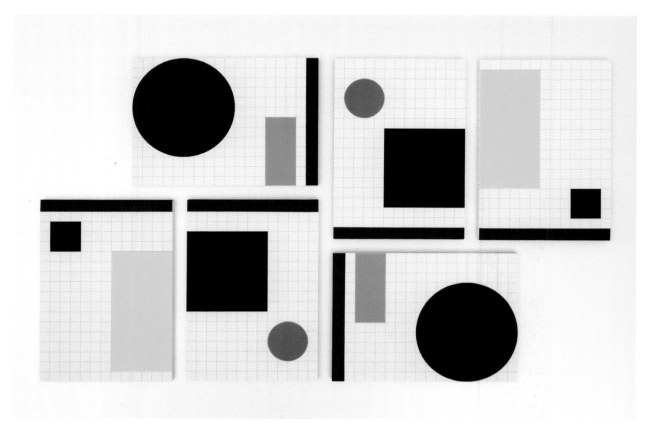

ODDFISCHLEIN
HUB FOR DESIGN & PLAY

HUB for Design & Play is an exploratory project managed by the Design School Kolding, seeking to study how we can use play in all kinds of processes and learning situations. Danish play design is internationally known and recognized for its functional, thought-out, stimulating and "playfully simple" play experiences – experiences that are created for and with children. User involvement is also widely used in the design profession, where awareness about involving users in the design process is the starting point for creating a good product.'

To create a playful visual platform for the project, the team at Danish corporate design studio OddFischlein referenced childhood classics, geometric knock-sets and blocks. For partner and graphic designer Klaus Matthiesen, the colourful geometric designs 'can merge into multiple, even endless variations. both abstract and figurative' – much like play itself.

Publisher Designskolen Kolding, Design2Innovate
Art Direction Klaus Matthiesen (OddFischlein)
Design Lars Johansen
Production WeProduce
Origin Denmark

ATIPO
GEOMANIST BOOKLET

The Geomanist booklet is a series of three inspirational, soft-cover books, housed in a black box with glossy, black-stamped typography. An overview of the Geomanist typeface, it was developed by Spanish graphic design studio Atipo, whose work is centred around the discipline 'geometry and rhythm'.

The three books are distinguishable by their bold geometric covers which feature a single black circle, square and triangle printed onto three different Colorplan paper stocks (harvest, turquoise and mandarin).

The clean and elegant books are a showcase for the graphic capabilities of the new typeface, and feature original compositions that visualize different musical themes and song quotes to highlight the humanistic beat of the typeface.

Art Direction & Design Atipo
Production Minke
Origin Spain

ANYMADE STUDIO
THE TRICKLING EXPANSE

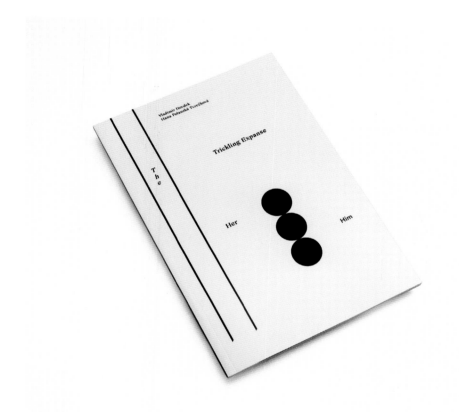

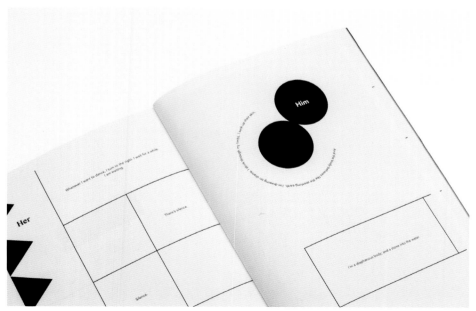

The Trickling Expanse is a collaborative art-film collage between Prague-based artist Vladimír Houdek and dancer Hana Polanská Turečková. The film, inspired by Houdek's eponymous poem, and supporting book published by the Polansky Gallery in Prague, seeks to create a correspondence between painting and body language.

The book features film stills that portray Houdek's geometric black-and-white paintings interspersed with choreographed dancing shots and graphic representations of the original poem that were intentionally rearranged by Anymade Studio, a graphic design studio in Prague. They are deliberately intended to make the poem harder to read. As Petr Cabalka, founder of Anymade Studio, explains, 'We were inspired by the paintings of artist Vladimír Houdek. We knew that his work is full of references to modernism and the avant-garde. His (libretto) poem is especially hard to read and we decided to make it even more complicated to read, even though the new composition is a lot easier for random reads because of the new relationships between characters.'

Publisher Polansky Gallery
Art Direction Anymade Studio, Jiří Havlíček
Design Filip Nerad, Petr Cabalka (Anymade Studio)
Illustration Hana Polanská Turečková, Anymade Studio
Production Tiskárna Helbich, a.s.
Origin Czech Republic

&LARRY
FRAGMENTS OF GREY MATTER

Fragments of Grey Matter is a quarter-bound book that collates images created by the Hong Kong-born photographic artist Kristin Man over a period of two years.

It reflects Man's desire to create images that straddle the absolute and the abstract as she attempts to find beauty and meaning in-between. The title reflects this concept on two levels: a reference to cerebral grey matter, suggesting the emotional nature of her images, and the vacillation between concrete and abstract, beautiful and not-so-beautiful.

The geometric cover design, created by Singapore-based graphic design studio &Larry, uses deliberately thick board, which was die-cut through one signature layer and works as a visual and material reference to the human head.

Creative Direction Larry Peh (&Larry)
Design Randy Yeo
Photography Kristin Man
Production Colourscan
Origin Singapore

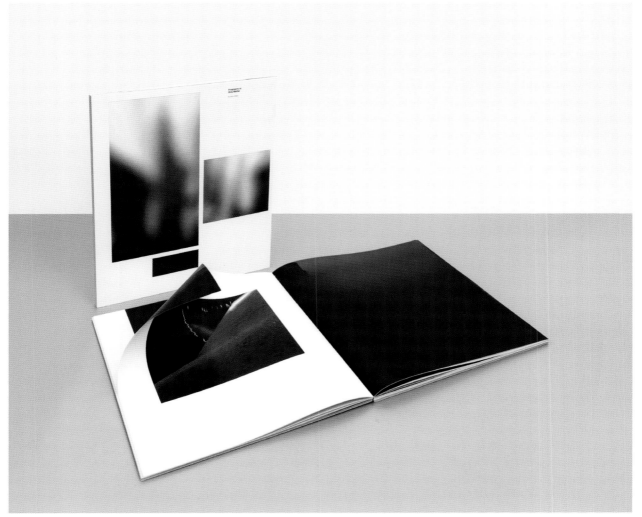

NOUVELLE ADMINISTRATION
MOLTO PIANO, JAZZ EN RAFALE

Established in 2000 by the non-profit organization Jazz Services, the annual Jazz en Rafale festival in Montreal highlights the 'very best in contemporary piano jazz' and brings jazz artists from around the world together with local, Quebec-based musicians.

The Italian musical term *molto* means 'very' and is used with other musical notations to intensify an effect. The festival announced its intention for the 2014 season with the title 'Molto Piano'. To create the new visual identity to accompany the season, the Montreal-based studio Nouvelle Administration (then called La Mamzelle & Co.) developed what they describe as an 'abstract play of positive and negative space, creating a playful grid'. Getting to the core

of the festival, the team said, 'we wanted to graphically create a syncopated beat. We felt that the brand should capture the improvisational aesthetic and dynamic rhythms of jazz'. Fittingly, one inspiration for this project was Piet Mondrian's 1943 painting *Broadway Boogie-Woogie*.

With a nod to the charitable status of the festival, the creative team at Nouvelle Administration acknowledge that the budget for the campaign was always going to be limited. 'We had to keep costs at a minimum, yet achieve a high level of effectiveness. During the process, it became evident we did not need colour.'

Art Direction & Design Éloïse Deschamps, Martin Poirier (Nouvelle Administration)
Origin Canada

HELLOME
WARP RECORDS

For 25 years, the UK-based electronic music label Warp Records have been releasing explorative music created by artists Aphex Twin, Flying Lotus, Brian Eno, Hudson Mohawke and Squarepusher.

The quarter-of-a-century milestone triggered a refresh of the brand identity, and Berlin-based graphic design studio HelloMe were commissioned to create an extensive repositioning of the label's brand identity.

In close collaboration with Warp Records, an adaptive geometric design system was developed to meet the complexities of today's print and digital environment. The new identity system, featuring the iconic purple which has been central to the label's identity since its inception, was developed. It utilized a flexible grid system that was designed to host multiple content on varying applications, from magazine adverts to responsive websites, developed by London-based Stinkdigital.

A complete typographic overhaul was developed to accompany the rebrand. It was created in collaboration with the type foundry Dinamo, who expanded the typeface 'Favorit' by including Warp-specific icons and custom glyphs.

The final geometric design and adaptive grid structure is a crisp reinterpretation of Warp Records' identity cementing its position as one of the most creative independent record labels in the world.

Publisher Warp Records
Art Direction & Design Till Wiedeck (HelloMe)
Web Development Stinkdigital
Origin UK

HEY
ARTFAD

The Arts and Design Promotion is a Spanish not-for-profit association founded in 1903. It aims to promote regional design and architecture in cultural and economic life. The ArtFAD award represents the different disciplines of design: industrial, graphic, architecture, interior, arts, craft and fashion, fostering creative culture through a series of exhibitions, talks and events.

Each year the awarding body commissions a graphic identity; recently Barcelona-based graphic design studio Hey were commissioned. The studio produced a series of bold, geometric designs centred on the letter A, which is rendered differently each year. For the 2013 event, Hey created a series of 500 hand-constructed invitations that reference the party flags.

Art Direction Hey
Production Grafiko, Hey
Origin Spain

EDITED
ISHOKU ORANGE

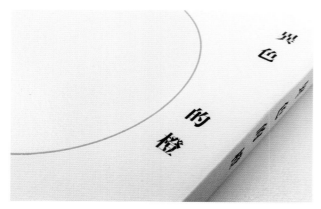

Ishoku Orange is a series of 'mini novels' – tales of love and desire, dreams and imagination, poetry and illustrations.

For the cover design, Edited wanted to hint at the world inside the book. The 'ishoku orange' itself is a mysterious symbol for the whole book. The main character squeezes and breaks the orange at the end of the story. The cover does not reveal much of the content, but readers will find its linkage with the stories when they have finished reading. The cover gives the readers an entrance to a world that is quirky and fragmented.

The designer also used a circular form to link with the other elements in the book: the circle echoes the illustration on the first and last insert, which are distorted images of a female figure.

Publisher Kubrick
Art Direction Renatus Wu (Edited)
Illustration Wongszechit
Production Sun Wah Printing Factory Limited
Origin Hong Kong

夏芝然

異色

的橙

迷你小說

WARD HEIRWEGH
HET PAVILJOEN

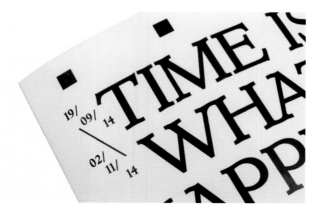

Het Paviljoen is an independent centre for experimental art founded by the Royal Academy of Fine Arts (KASK), the Higher Institute for Fine Arts (HISK) and the Museum of Contemporary Art (SMAK), all in Ghent. The contemporary space, encased in glass, appoints a new artistic coordinator for each exhibition to further the artistic growth of future talent.

The graphic identity differs for each original exhibition and is created by Antwerp-based graphic designer Ward Heirwegh. The distinct glass structure provided inspiration for the graphic identity, which features square blocks that map out the solid architectural points that define the space – the metal beams that hold all the glass. A different colour palette is assigned to each exhibition to create a simplified flexible design structure. As Heirwegh explains, 'As a graphic designer, I tried to view the project also as an object, just as the curator does. The floor plan translated itself into this set of squares which can then be used to "house" the typography. It's a very flexible and open system. You can stretch it over surfaces, exchange the squares for other shapes, change typography… as long as you keep the grid and distances between the points.'

Art Direction & Design Ward Heirwegh
Origin Belgium

VILLAGE GREEN
ALPHABETA

European real-estate investors Resolution Property have redeveloped a landmark building in Finsbury Square, London, turning it into 'Alphabeta', a modern working environment for the creative and technology sectors. Resolution commissioned the London-based creative agency Village Green to help tell the visual story of this giant architectural and commercial project.

Village Green took on branding, identity, digital and moving-image assets, as well as the interior design for the marketing suite, which included a gallery space, video projections, architectural model design, signage and wayfinding.

Reflecting on the design process, designer Peter Richardson says, 'The building is presented as a physical meeting point between the traditions of the City and the expanding creative influences of Shoreditch. The geometric colour designs are applied to represent this cross-over, with interactions that emphasize a bold visual dynamic – a metaphor for the "tech-city" industries that are emerging in the local area.'

Art Direction & Design Village Green
Photography Nick Guttridge, Matt Chisnall
Production Opal Print
Origin UK

LEO BURNETT
CREATIVE CIRCLE UK

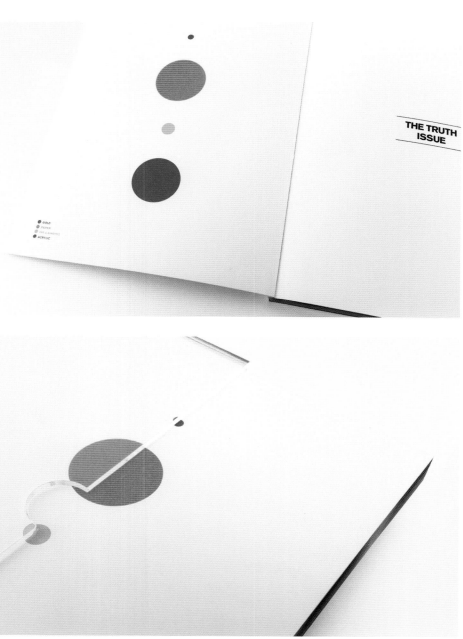

Creative Circle, the oldest advertising and marketing awarding body in Europe, celebrated its 70th anniversary in 2015. It is also an educational body, run and developed by practising creatives, which aims to get those at the top of their profession to help those just starting out to improve their creative practice: an unending cycle of support.

Each year they publish one magazine, which showcases winning and shortlisted entries to the awards scheme, but also features a raft of new content created around a central, usually one-word, theme. In 2015 the theme was 'truth', and creatives from around the world were invited to submit work interpreting this subject, with the best entries featured in the editorial section.

For Marc Donaldson and Tim Fletcher at Leo Burnett Design, the brief was to create a celebratory showcase, but one that, importantly, stood out from similar publications. The duo reflect upon their approach to the design: 'We decided to explore the physical "truths" of the annual itself; superfluous elements and embellishment were removed from the cover and we used uncoated stock and blind embossing for the type. The front of the annual only features four brightly coloured circles: three on the cover and one on the perspex case.'

Each circle represents a different part of the magazine and the size and weight of the circle further reveals a truth about each element, in a kind of exploded pie chart: pink represents the paper, yellow the ink and binding, blue the acrylic, and gold the coveted top awards themselves.

Publisher Creative Circle UK
Executive Creative Director Justin Tindall
Creative Direction & Design Marc Donaldson, Tim Fletcher (Leo Burnett Design)
Production Podigious/Connekt
Origin UK

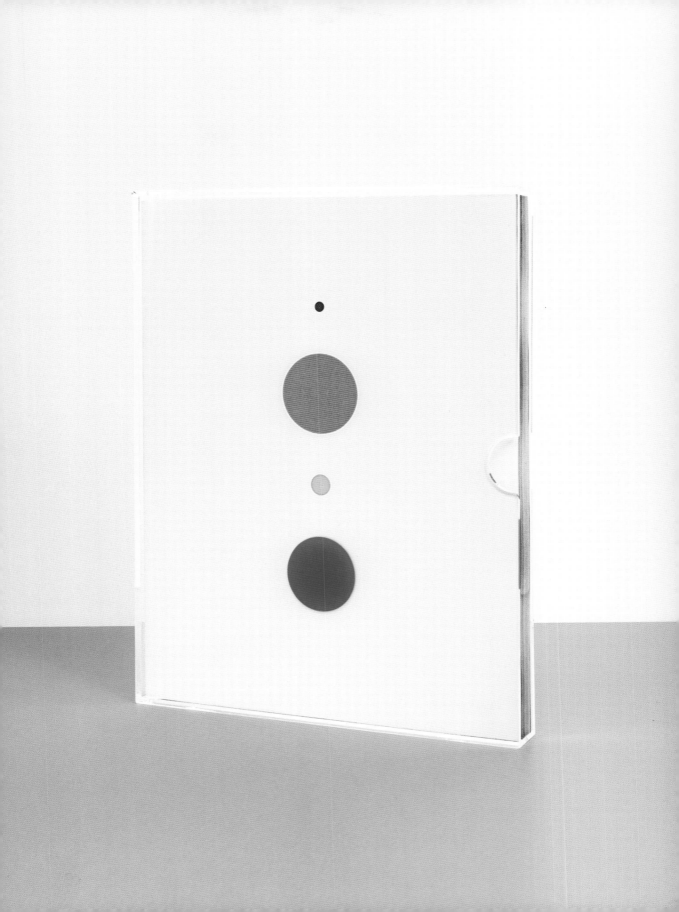

NEO NEO
AMARCORDES

Les Concerts Amarcordes are an annual programme of live classical music performed in the evocative setting of Dardagny Castle in Switzerland.

The Geneva-based design studio Neo Neo, jointly led by Thuy-An Hoang and Xavier Erni, have been working with Amarcordes since 2011. Over this period, the creative team have developed a strong formula that underpins all visual communications and now defines the concerts' entire visual identity:

'Two colours, geometric forms and a small-size, one-weight grotesque typeface is the formula.'

For Neo Neo, 'The simple geometric aesthetic is a kind of tribute to Swiss modernist graphic designers like Josef Müller Brockmann, Karl Gerstner and Armin Hoffman. We intend to visually represent the music through abstract forms.'

Publisher Les Concerts Amarcordes
Art Direction & Design Thuy-An Hoang, Xavier Erni (Neo Neo)
Production Imprimerie Villière
Origin Switzerland

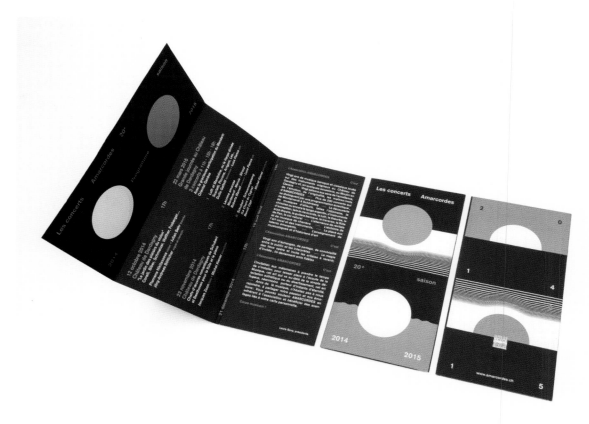

PLAYTYPE
NON-OBJECTIVE POSTER

The Copenhagen brand and design agency e-Types established their own online type foundry in 2010. Playtype create custom-made typefaces for brands and corporations and make a library of fonts available to individuals and graphic studios all over the world. They have a store and an online type foundry.

Unsurprisingly, the creative team state that, 'Typography is always the key ingredient in our design but we continually expand and explore the way we use and perceive type.' Their own Non-Objective series of four posters was created purely as 'an experiment with typographic compositions and colours'. The title of the poster series announces their intentions: non-objective means abstract or non-representational art that does not represent or depict a person, place or thing in the natural world.' Playtype continues, 'We wanted to emphasize the beauty found in the shapes of type, rather than emphasize any meaning of the letters. For us, it's all about the simplicity and beauty of type.'

Publisher Playtype
Art Direction & Design Playtype
Production Cool Gray
Origin Denmark

BAXTER AND BAILEY
UAL AWARDING BODY

University of the Arts London (UAL) is the only specialist organization in England that gives awards for the art, design and creative industries. They design, develop and award qualifications within the national qualifications framework. For Matt Baxter and Dom Bailey, who together are Baxter and Bailey design studio, to create a new visual identity for the organization meant digging deep. Simplicity of use was key and so 'to help us understand their world, we conducted interviews with art and design institutions around the country, as well as with UAL staff.'

Their design solution is boldly geometric and colourful. It is striking but it also performs another function: 'We chose colour and shape to form an overarching identity system. This allowed us to create a range of printed and digital communications for a variety of courses, at different levels of qualification, without relying on the imagery of specific creative disciplines.' It's a strong, simple visual solution for a complex world, with a triangle, square and circle standing for educational attainment levels 4, 3 and 2 and different colour treatments across creative disciplines.

Client UAL Awarding Body
Art Direction Matt Baxter, Dom Bailey (Baxter and Bailey)
Design Matt Baxter, Dom Bailey, Graeme Rodrigo, Jessica Philpott
Production Gavin Martin Colournet, MTA Digital
Origin UK

ual: university of the arts london awarding body

Diploma in Art & Design
- Foundation Studies

Level 3 and Level 4
–
Centre Handbook

Foundation

Centres

ual: university of the arts london awarding body

Award and Diploma
in Art & Design

Level 2
–
Centre Handbook

Art & Design

BVD
7-ELEVEN

When Stockholm-based studio BVD rebranded the Swedish 7-Eleven in-store coffee offerings in 2013 it caused quite a stir. The convenience store brand has become ubiquitous since its launch in 1927, but it is hardly known for cutting-edge graphic design.

BVD embraced the fact that the Swedish 7-Eleven wanted to change customer perceptions and move towards a more modern and urban feel. 'The challenge was to find a way to work within the existing, recognizable visual identity of 7-Eleven and yet modernize it. Our aim was to create a design that is long-lasting, fits with the new strategic position and which we can develop further within the store concept.'

BVD started with the most recognizable elements of the exisiting 7-Eleven brand: the stripes and colours. But from here they went on to create something stripped-back, bold and modern, adapting the colour palette and ramping up the speedy stripes across all the cups, bags and packaging. For them, the design captures the key elements of buying a quick coffee while on the move by balancing 'speed and straightforwardness with warmth and friendliness. It communicates in a clear and straightforward way, with an urban touch. It breaks through.'

Publisher Reitan Convenience
Art Directio & Design BVD
Production Tingstad
Origin Sweden

STUDIO FNT
KAYWON UNIVERSITY OF ART AND DESIGN

The Fact Book for Kaywon University of Art and Design celebrates the Korean institution's 20-year history. The tome consists of the university's educational goals and background, documenting its growth and change as an institution, and contains current information on facilities, course structures and student life. For Jaemin Lee, creative director of the Seoul-based Studio FNT, it was important to 'keep a timeless identity so the book wouldn't look too outdated or too trendy, even in another 20 years.' Lee turned to geometric shapes and simple typography. Aware, too, that the book contained disparate material, Lee noted, 'We needed a strong visual tool to tie all the varied content together. We used basic, fundamental forms and shapes to develop the overall look.'

Publisher Kaywon University of Art and Design
Art Direction Jaemin Lee, Heesun Kim (Studio FNT)
Design Hwayoung Lee, Jaemin Lee
Editor Heesun Kim
Production Chung San Printing Company
Origin Korea

QUIM MARIN
SALA PASTERNAK

Quim Marin is a Barcelona-based art director with a passion for mathematics and geometry in graphic design. He was commissioned by Sala Pasternak, a concert hall in Barcelona, to create a series of posters to advertise their forthcoming indie nights. His aim was to create a series that reflected the rhythm of the music events. 'Rhythm generally means a movement marked by the regulated succession of strong and weak elements, or of opposite or different conditions. I have tried to reflect this with colours, forms, contrast and tensions in the graphic design.'

Publisher Sala Pasternak
Art Direction Quim Marin
Origin Spain

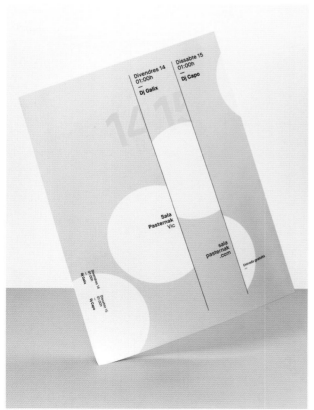

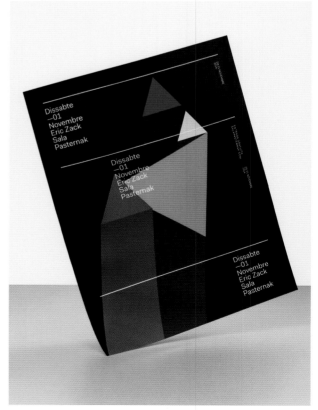

DOSSIER
14—15
—

10È
ANIVERSARI
—

10º
ANIVERSARIO
—

salapasternak
.com

SALA
PASTER
NAK—

MARK GOWING
DEEP MAGIC

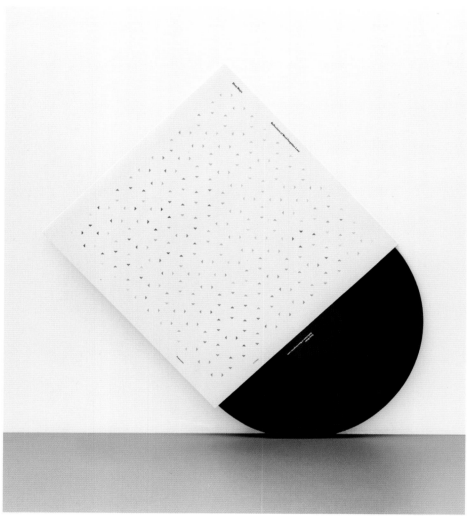

This is the third album from the Los Angeles-based musician and producer Alex Gray, who records his solo works under the name Deep Magic. Released by the Australian record label Preservation, they describe the album's soundscape as 'skittish techno, rolling pianos, warm pedal steel, foggy, dub drifts and microscopic sonics playing out a hypnotic movement of moods with magnetic compulsion.'

For the Sydney-based designer Mark Gowing, a long-term collaborator with the Preservation label, his design for the vinyl release 'represents the meditative, ambient, cosmic sound' of the album. It's a deconstructed mosaic typographic piece that is actually an abstraction of the album title *Reflections of Most Forgotten Love*. Gowing explains, 'The album title was typeset on a square grid using only triangles. The triangle mosaic was then deconstructed by adding negative space between each form as though the music had infected the canvas and was visually pushing the rhythm around.'

Publisher Preservation
Art Direction & Design Mark Gowing
Origin Australia

YUTA TAKAHASHI
TRINITY

Michael Debus is a theologian. He visited Japan in 2013 and in 2014, wanting to explain his own theory of the Holy Trinity to a new audience. He has written two books, *Trinity*, volumes 1 and 2, which capture his experiences in Japan and bring his theories to life.

To help understand the Trinity as the Father, the Son and the Holy Spirit, Debus refers us to duality. In the physical sciences, duality is the quality of being capable of exchange or interchange and even exisiting in two different states at the same time. Debus writes in volume 1 that he felt he 'failed' to explain this abstract concept on his tour of Japan and so he tries to advance the idea of dualism in his books.

The Japanese designer Yuta Takahashi tries visually to conceptualize the complex notion of duality at the heart of the book in his treatment. His response is a 'switch' motif, as he explains: 'When Japanese people publish a series of two books, we call volume 1 "Joh", which means upper part, and volume 2 "Ge", which means lower part. I applied to the spines an abstract image of a switch, in the positions of "on" and "off". For the cover, I used a cross and triangle to represent the Holy Trinity.' Using black and white further underscores the idea of duality.

Publisher Die Christengemeinschaft
Art Direction & Design Yuta Takahashi
Origin Japan

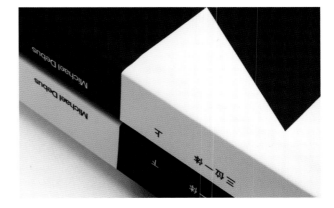

MADE THOUGHT
COLORPLAN

Colorplan is a range of paper with 50 colours, 25 embossings and eight weights made by UK paper manufacturer G . F Smith. To promote the range, a series of books and teaser packs were released which highlight the expressive qualities of the paper.

The refresh of the Colorplan range was led by London-based graphic design studio Made Thought, whose first task was to look at the existing logo, set in Helvetica. An important aspect of the original brief was to 'set the foundations for the brand to grow', which was realized in the development of a new Color Book typeface. It is accompanied by a Colorplan brand mark referencing a physical sheet of paper turned up at the corner, a traditional method for marking a page for reference. The purpose of the brand mark was to maximize the range and reveal other layers, thus providing the opportunity to showcase the colours available.

A 200-page notebook, featuring all 50 Colorplan colours, was produced with perforated pages to encourage designers to tear out pages for notes or colour samples for project reference. Five print techniques were used, including lithography, digital printing, foil blocking, embossing and thermography; it is bound using a traditional section-sewn technique, which is left exposed.

Alongside the two Color Books, a concertina format swatch booklet was developed, featuring a die-cut geometric circle design and a Colorplan teaser pack which consists of 50 coloured circles housed in a hand-made translucent envelope.

The series is an effortlessly simple, bright range of promotional materials that concentrate on the expressive qualities inherent in the paper rather than focusing on its technical attributes.

Publisher G . F Smith
Art Direction & Design Made Thought
Origin UK

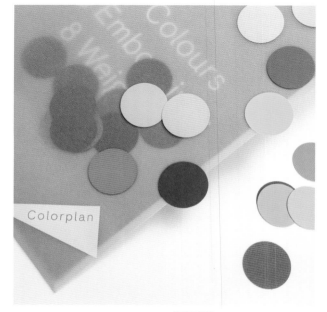

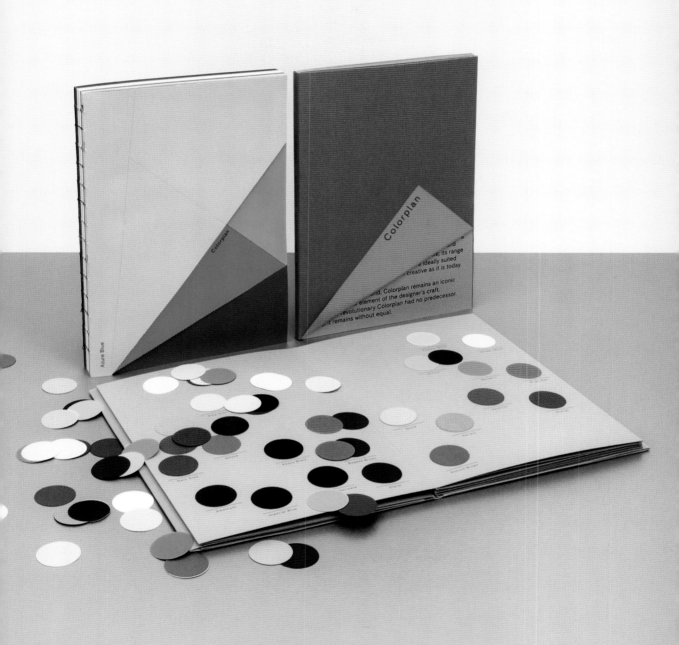

PENG HSING KAI
WHAT NOW

Published by Yuan-Liou in Taiwan, *What Now* by Lin Xi is a metaphor for the author's inward-looking style of writing.

The minimalist cover design features a semi-colon printed in black hot foil, which is a playful interpretation of Lin Xi's internal writing style. As Peng Hsing Kai, the book cover designer, explains, 'When you look at the cover directly, it might be elegant, aloof and sensitive, but if you rotate it 90 degrees it becomes a cute and funny face. It's a metaphor for the author's projected social image and the inwardness of his writing.'

Printed in two formats, white paperback and gold hardback, with paper options supplied by the Sincere Paper Company (for the paperback) and Yuen Foong Paper Company (for the hardback), the black hot-foil details create a soft non-aggressive design.

Publisher Yuan-Liou Publishing Co.,Ltd.
Art Direction & Design Peng Hsing Kai
Origin Taiwan

MARIUS JOPEN
LOVE REVOLUTION

On 27 June 2014, Goleb, an artist-led space located on the second floor of a former school building in Amsterdam's New-West, hosted the first edition of 'Love Revolution'. The event is a collaboration between the Love Foundation, an open network of students, activists and artists who collectively generate money in order to provide clean drinking water and sanitary installations to the people living in rural Bihar, India, and the Amsterdam-based electronic music platform Revolutziya.

The creation of promotional posters adorned with bold geometric patterns, a reduced colour palette and deconstructed typography was created by Marius Jopen, an Amsterdam-based graphic designer and one of three founders of the Love Foundation. The posters feature visual references to Swiss graphic design, a style that originated in Switzerland in the 1940s and 1950s, as a method to visualize the electronic music. As Jopen explains, 'I was inspired by the classic Swiss graphic design and tried to translate it into a more modern, dark, electronic vibe. The strokes symbolize the rhythm of the music.'

Publisher Love Foundation
Art Direction & Design Marius Jopen
Origin The Netherlands

FARROW
PET SHOP BOYS

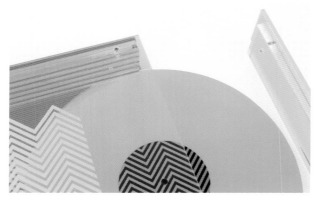

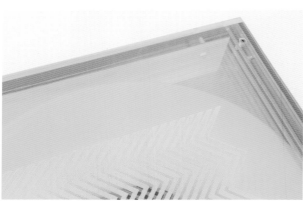

Farrow, the London-based studio founded by art director Mark Farrow, has enjoyed a long-standing working relationship with the Pet Shop Boys that began in the 1980s. Farrow continues to work with Neil Tennant and Chris Lowe, and his minimalist visual direction has become synonymous with their clean electronic sound.

For the duo's 12th studio album, *Electric*, Farrow created a zig-zag design that hints at the *Electric* album title and reflects the band's dance-orientated approach to music production while adhering to their request not to appear on the cover.

A set of rules was applied to the design, which was only printed in a single colour, with no title type. An important consideration was that the design needed to work over a number of formats, especially in today's digital landscape.

Farrow explains, 'Most people now view album images on the screen of a mobile device which renders complicated designs or photographic images almost useless. For this album, and *Yes*, released in 2009, we created album identities rather than individual covers as they are normally perceived.'

The identity was rendered in a fluorescent explosion on the live tour book and the *Electric* box set, which was created in collaboration with The Vinyl Factory, a London-based music and art specialist. This art edition is a multi-coloured box set containing five fluorescent-coloured 180-gram vinyl records, limited to just 350 copies worldwide.

An electric blue was chosen for the standard edition vinyl because the album was called *Electric*. This worked alongside the zig-zag pattern, which started as a lightning bolt and became the pattern that you now see on the cover.

Publisher x2, The Vinyl Factory
Art Direction Farrow, Pet Shop Boys
Design Mark Farrow, Gary Stillwell, Fred Ross
Production The Vinyl Factory
Origin UK

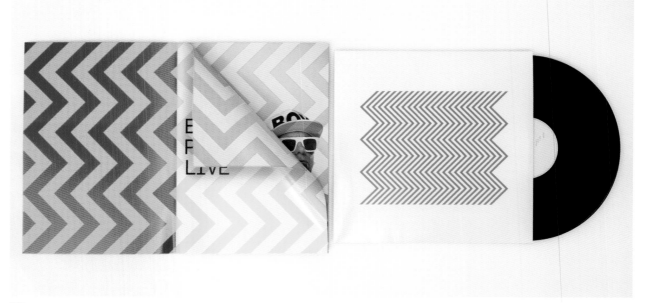

BLOK
CEE (COALITION FOR ENGAGED EDUCATION)

Based in Toronto, Blok are a multi-disciplinary studio, working with clients from around the world.

The Coalition for Engaged Education (CEE) are a non-profit organization in Los Angeles who help the most vulnerable youths in society realize their potential through an education programme that ignites and inspires them. Dr Paul Cummins, a celebrated educator and the founder of CEE, invited Blok to create a new brand identity to signal the coalition's intent.

In Vanessa Eckstein and Marta Cutler's words, 'Coalition for Engaged Education is a long name. We embraced its acronym, CEE, and recommended that this be the primary identifier. However, we recognized it was critical that the new identity reflect not only the organization but also the students themselves. They needed to feel part of the brand story and to quite literally wear the new identity with pride.'

The resulting logo is a combination of formal sans-serif typography and a minimalist geometric icon. The circular shapes reference the rounded forms of CEE in a palette of bold, bright colours juxtaposed with subtle blues and browns that capture the joy found in the organization's work.

Art Direction Vanessa Eckstein, Marta Cutler (Blok)
Design Vanessa Eckstein, Miki Arai, Kevin Boothe
Production Flash Reproductions
Origin Canada

LA TIGRE
ARCARREDA

Based in Milan, Arcarreda design and manufacture household furnishings and interiors that adhere to the traditional Scandinavian style of design.

Milan-based graphic design studio La Tigre, renowned for their illustrative graphic design style and clean colour palette, created an identity design that reflected the vintage nature of the furniture manufacturer with a playful and abstract use of a mono-spaced typeface. As creative partner Luisa Milani explains,

'Our proposal for the identity is complex and based on three levels of interpretation. The "hidden" level is a grid-based design that abstracts a sans-serif mono-spaced font and features cropped stationery to create contemporary graphic detail that complements the Arcarreda serif logotype.' The combination of all three levels creates a clean modern geometric identity.

Art Direction & Design La Tigre
Origin Italy

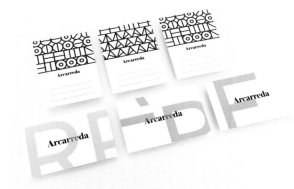

BUNCH
KODE

A collective of creative producers and directors, Kode Media are a video production company working out of London and New York. In 2014, they launched a sub-brand, Kode Red, and commissioned London-based design studio Bunch to develop new visual identities.

Bunch teamed up with Sebazzo, a digital design studio, to create a website that showcases the best of Kode's work. Both teams had to respond to a brief that was 'simple and grounded', according to Sebazzo, to create a site that focuses on the best of Kode Media's work – a large portfolio of digital content, from music promos to commercial advertising. For Sebazzo, the Kode–Kode Red split was addressed 'through a simple tab device on the top left of the page, allowing users to make a clear choice between the two very different types of content at any stage during their visit.'

Denis Kovac, the creative director at Bunch, agrees that 'simplicity was the key.' The new logo had to work across all kinds of printed collateral. 'We focused on a simple word mark with an element of code to reflect the brand name. The logo takes the angle of "K" to make the opening bracket and uses it as an abstract "D" for the closing bracket. At the same time, the word is intended to work as a symbol, with an image of a "hidden eye" within – an eye being a mark that refers to Kode's creative vision.'

Art Direction & Design Bunch
Production Cerovski
Origin UK

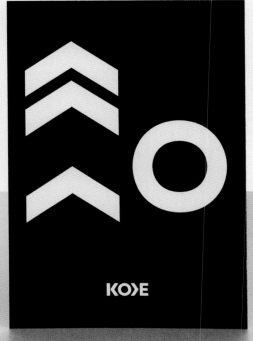

PETER GREGSON STUDIO
DJURDJIC WINERY

Djurdjic Winery are a Serbian wine producer set up in the region of Sremski Karlovci in 2004. Their vineyard has views of the Danube that have probably remained unchanged across the centuries, but they themselves look firmly to the future, as one of the youngest growers in the region.

The Peter Gregson Studio (PGS), based in Novi Sad in Serbia, were asked to create a new visual identity. The creative director, Jovan Trkulja, reflects on the relative youthfulness of the brand and how this shaped his response to the brief: 'Djurdjic Winery does not have a strong heritage background and so we were free to create a simplified design which represents the winery as it sees itself, as new and bold.'

The team at PGS use flat, extensive panels of colour in bold shades, bordered and accentuated by white. Some of the colour choices were informed by the wine itself. 'The Bermet wine is designed with black stripes because of its name: Crni vitez, or Black Knight.'

A silver block-foiled shield on each bottle hints at heritage, but the creative team has dispensed with any of the other illustrative details commonly seen in the wine industry. The mono-spaced type brings a technical feel to the label, which echoes the winery's modern production methods.

Publisher Djurdjic Winery
Art Direction Jovan Trkulja (Peter Gregson Studio)
Design Jovan Trkulja, Milica Pantelić
Production ProMedia
Origin Serbia

KIM HIORTHØY
RUNE GRAMMOFON

The Rune Grammofon record label only releases work by 'the most adventurous and creative Norwegian artists and composers'. Each release is created with care and attention, aiming to recapture the magic of record-hunting in the digital age. This dedication extends to their long-standing relationship with Norwegian designer Kim Hiorthøy, who creates their abstract, often heavily geometric cover designs. For Rune Kristoffersen at Rune Grammofon, 'It's only a part of Kim's graphic language, so I wouldn't say it's more important than other directions.... It has never been an intention that the covers should reflect the music. If anything, they will often have some kind of connection to the album title or a song title.... In principle, Kim has total artistic freedom when it comes to sleeve design. He will get the music and the titles and work from that.'

Publisher Rune Grammofon
Art Direction & Design Kim Hiorthøy
Production Optimal Media
Origin Norway

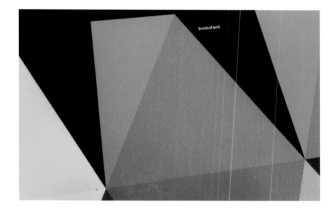

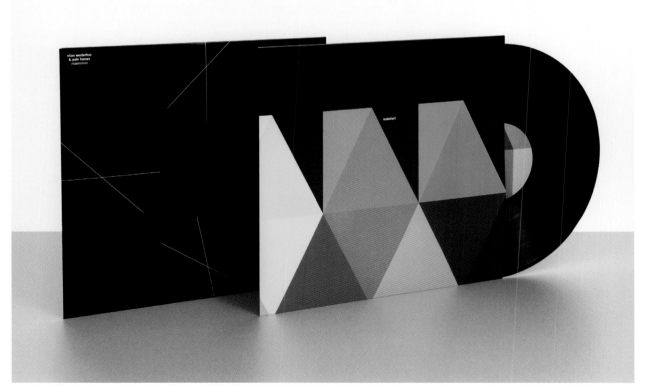

FACE
RMFF

The Riviera Maya Film Festival (RMFF) brings the best of national and international cinema to Quintana Roo in Mexico. RMFF commissioned Face to develop a fresh graphic concept for their third annual event.

Rik Bracho, creative director at Face – a self-described 'supermodernist' design studio based in the same Monterrey area as the festival – says that he used 'geometry and a vintage, fresh colour palette to generate an aesthetic language based on simplicity and the union of shapes and people. We have graphically represented the famous sunsets of the Riviera Maya. The design is driven by connection, using a modular graphic system. I think it's a modern yet classy style.'

It was an important project for Bracho. 'Mexico is a very complex country, and in some places design, well, good design is almost absent. That's why we wanted to create something based on simplicity, something strong, easy to adapt, easy to understand, and above all beautiful. Geometry is one of the purest forms of communication, and it's an amazing tool for design. It was a no-brainer to solve this message with a graphic theme that reflected the Mayan Riviera, the sunset and the feeling of something fresh, yet nostalgic.'

Publisher The Riviera Maya Film Festival (RMFF)
Art Direction Rik Bracho (Face)
Design Rik Bracho, Cristina Vila Nadal
Origin Mexico

rmff
riviera maya film festival
2014

www.rmff.mx

3a Edición
9 — 15 Marzo 2014

El cine _____ nos une

RAY O'MEARA
THE WHITE REVIEW

The White Review is a London quarterly arts journal published in print and online which specializes in 'artistically or educationally meritorious works of new or emerging artists and writers'. With the promotion of arts and literature at its heart, it takes not only its name but a degree of inspiration from *La Revue Blanche*. The Parisian magazine ran from 1889 to 1903 and featured contributions from some of the greatest visual and literary artists of the era, including Pierre Bonnard, Marcel Proust and Paul Verlaine.

Ray O'Meara is the creative force behind the print version. He runs his own design studio, The Office of Optimism, which states a commitment to 'craftsmanship, simplicity and balance'. He says of his work for *The White Review*

that it is 'designed with clarity and classical simplicity in mind'. The journal format gives a solid structure with room for surprise, as O'Meara explains: 'From the outset it was designed as a series, one that features emerging and established artists of all disciplines side by side, but with each issue presenting a different artist on the cover.' O'Meara makes good use of production techniques: 'The cover itself acts as both a dust jacket and a fold-out poster'. Inside the pages are typographically led layouts, which accompany visual essays.

Publisher The White Review
Art Direction Ray O'Meara
Design The Office of Optimism
Cover Art Franziska Holstein, Mai-Thu Perret, Andrew Brischler
Production Push
Origin UK

STEPHEN PARKER
THE METAPHYSICS OF PING-PONG

The Metaphysics of Ping-Pong by Guido Mina di Sospiro depicts the author's metaphysical journey of self-discovery through the art of table tennis. As such, it clearly could not just look like any other book about the sport. As cover designer Stephen Parker explains, 'It needed a very graphic solution, and one that would make the reader think, in the same way as the writing.'

Parker began with the sport's basic constituents: ball, net, paddles and table; he decided not even to think about the player, as this would, of course, be the reader. After working out that championship games are played on blue tables, not the muddy green of youth clubs and school common rooms, and that the paddles are usually red or black, it was then just a matter of playing with the three basic colours.

'Taking the pure white sphere of the ball as my starting point, I wondered if the design could actually be based purely on circles. The tips of the paddles appear to be semi-circular, so we imagine the rest of the paddle shape even though they are perfect circles which continue round onto the flap of the jacket.

The spine of the book itself gave the opportunity to suggest the net with a simple white strip: just enough to indicate that it is a two-sided game. Having arrived at a design which was abstract enough to convey the content of the book, I wanted to further simplify it by screen-printing it in its three pure colours. Spending a day at Ink Spot Press in Brighton, I finally managed to get a print which had the smooth texture I wanted and just the right colours to evoke the idea of ping-pong.'

Publisher Yellow Jersey Press
Art Direction Stephen Parker
Production CPI
Origin UK

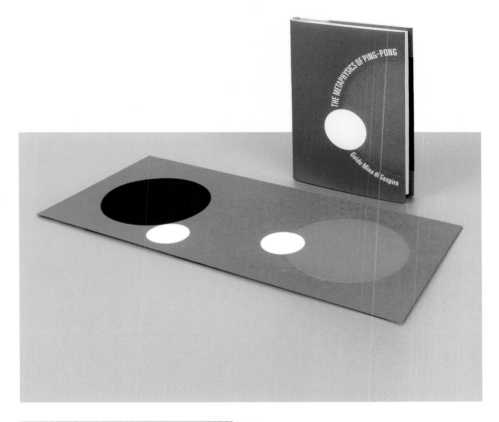

ENA CARDENAL DE LA NUEZ
THE SPANISH PROTECTORATE IN MOROCCO

This work marks the centenary of the installation of the Spanish Protectorate in Morocco, and sets out to analyse and explain this important period of shared history between the years 1912 and 1956. The hefty, three-volume publication gathers together the work of over 60 specialists from both countries to review the period from a contemporary perspective.

For Spanish designer Ena Cardenal de la Nuez it was this emphasis on a contemporary viewpoint that informed her whole approach to the book. 'I did not want to use images, which would provide a typical representation of history. Instead, I tried to announce the concept of the book with a non-representational, abstract visual language, using fonts and masses of colour'.

The book is 1,420 pages long, split into three volumes, housed in a slipcase. De la Nuez was able to use the physicality of the book to playful effect. 'On the jackets of the three volumes I combined masses of colour – blue, black, fuchsia, yellow, orange and grey – to build a set of triangles. When the three covers appear together, laid flat, they form a kind of drawing or tile.' It is an approach that subtly echoes both Moroccan and Mediterranean patterned tiles. De la Nuez notes further that 'These triangles also refer to the tips of a star, a fundamental symbol in Arabic culture and aesthetics.'

Publisher Iberdrola
Art Direction & Design Ena Cardenal de la Nuez
Production Cromotex, TF Artes Gráficas
Origin Spain

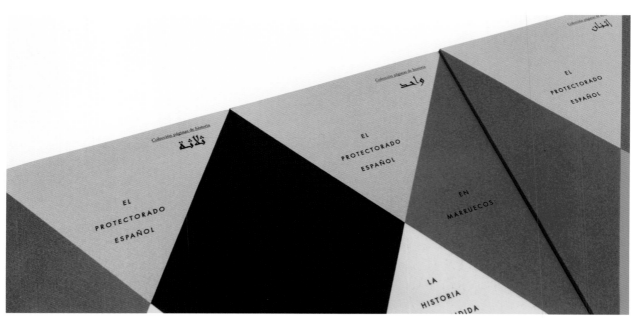